MIND, STRESS

By the same author

SOCIAL CAUSES OF ILLNESS
SOCIAL AND BIOLOGICAL ROLES OF LANGUAGE

MIND, STRESS AND HEALTH

Richard Totman

A CONDOR BOOK
SOUVENIR PRESS (E & A) LTD

ISBN 0 285 65085 8 hardback
ISBN 0 285 65090 4 paperback

Photoset in Great Britain by
Rowland Phototypesetting Ltd,
Bury St Edmunds, Suffolk
Printed in Great Britain by
Billing and Sons Ltd., Worcester

For Barb

CONTENTS

LIST OF FIGURES AND TABLES

FIGURES

TABLES

ACKNOWLEDGEMENTS

I thank Barbara Kugler, John Butt, Cathy Feeney, Raymond ffoulkes, Rona Davies and Felicity-Ann Totman for their helpful comments on a draft of this book.

For permission to reproduce copyright material I am grateful to: the *Lancet*, the *Social Affairs Unit*, *Macmillan Ltd.*, *Parthenon Publishing Group*, *Addison-Wesley*, *The Sunday Times*, Professor. A. Galvão-Teles, and *Scientific American*.

Rona Davies was responsible for the production of the Figures.

INTRODUCTION

The debate about diet and healthy eating is a fascinating one. There is a great deal of scientific research on the subject, and recommendations about what we should and should not eat are regularly put out with great confidence by medical authorities and government committees. The trouble is that these have a disconcerting habit of changing with time. The 'healthy' diet of the 1950s, for example, bears hardly any resemblance to the 'healthy' diet of today.

Is this because research on food and health has come a long way in the past few decades? There has been a tremendous amount of this research, including some expensive studies of very large groups of people, and it is undeniable that knowledge has advanced. But a careful assessment of the evidence reveals that there is little scientific backing to many of the recommendations about which foods are good or bad for you, even though some of these have come to be accepted as self-evident facts. I began looking at the literature mildly sceptical of what I had heard, but ended up frankly amazed at the man of straw—the inconsistencies and confusions—I found. Extravagant claims have been made for individual pieces of research that are not justified by the data. For example, a large American study carried out in the late 1970s and early 1980s, spanning seven years, involved a group of nearly 4,000 men with raised cholesterol in their blood. Its aim was to test the power of a drug, cholestyramine, to reduce blood cholesterol levels and prevent heart disease. Two groups were compared—one given the drug plus a special diet, the other given only the special diet. A difference between the two groups was found after seven years in blood cholesterol level and in incidence of heart disease.[1] On the basis of this finding, recommendations were made that everyone should change their diet, cutting down on saturated fats.[2] However, the experiment was not an experiment about diet at all—it was a drug trial. Finding a difference between the diet-plus-drug group and the diet-only group tells us nothing at all about the effect of the diet. Incidentally, although deaths through heart disease were reduced in the group receiving the drug, overall mortality (deaths from all causes combined) was not.

Inaccuracy and mistakes in the reporting of 'discoveries' about diet and health are very common: reports about good and bad foods enjoy such universal interest that news often takes over from fact. The first two chapters of this book demonstrate that there is no foundation for many of the claims made about the universally healthy diet; for most people these are inappropriate and for some they may even be dangerous. Panels and committees like nothing better than to issue statements about what people should and shouldn't do—indeed this is part of their function. But there can be no doubt that with regard to diet, the urge to prescribe and proscribe (especially the latter) has proved too much, and rhetoric has overtaken the careful weighing and reporting of facts.

While the first two chapters of the book explore the diet-health debate in some detail, this is not primarily a book about diet. It is about the psychological conditions of health and illness. Its thesis is that psychological factors, like stress, personality, and the support of other people, have profound effects on a person's physical health and survival: dietary factors, in comparison, by and large do not. Research into the effects of diet and drugs on health enjoys a much higher profile and level of funding than that into the effects of psychological state. Food and drugs are hard, tangible things that are easy to give or withhold, while 'psychological stress', 'support', etc., are often regarded as qualities too imprecise to be the subject-matter of proper science. I argue that while this may have been the case in the past, there is no longer any justification for holding such a view, and this bias in medicine must now be rejected as out-dated.

Research on diet and health has reached a kind of *impasse*. Since the stentorian pronouncements of the 1970s and early 1980s, governments and committees have become a shade more reticent: the latest statements are noticeably toned down.

In sharp contrast, evidence for the effects of personality and stress on health, illness and mortality has made some dramatic advances over the past decade, both empirically and theoretically. The most important of these concerns the effects of stress on the human immune system. We now know that the immune system is involved in the control of health in a very wide range of conditions, including cancer. We also know that there is an intimate system of communication between the brain and the immune system, and that the immune system is easily upset by hormones released in times of stress. There is now clear evidence that psychological states like depression, stress and the failure to cope with problems disable the immune system in various ways and interfere with its health-protecting function. Chapters 3 to 8 explore this recent evidence, contrasting it with the flimsy evidence concerning diet. The later chapters attempt to make sense of it by weaving it into a theory of the nature of stress and its relation to illness, and how we can avoid stress and stay well.

The aims of this book are therefore quite wide-ranging and this inevitably means there are omissions. There is no detailed discussion, for example, of the differences between men and women in susceptibility to the different forms of stress and illness. Most of the work on heart disease has been done with men, and this probably reflects a bias on the part of researchers and funders: heart disease kills many more men than women. There is no discussion of studies with animals or humans in which individuals are artificially subjected to stress in a laboratory. This omission is deliberate; the reason for it is summed up in a recent paper reviewing the effects of stress on the human immune system and cancer: 'The general feeling of those concerned has been that the effects of acute, experimental stress on the immune system are entirely different from the effects of prolonged, naturally occurring stress.'[3]

It has not been possible to provide a comprehensive account of every study done in every area of research referred to. In each area, hundreds, if not thousands, of studies have been published, and to list all these would be an insurmountable task and also a rather futile one. I have concentrated on the better designed and more recent studies representing the current state of our knowledge, making a special effort not to omit those that go against the argument. Indexed at points along the text are key references to good recent reviews of each topic.

A preliminary caution must be added concerning the term 'risk factor'. This is a term widely used in the medical literature and unfortunately it can be a misleading one. For instance, there are five main risk factors for heart disease: age, sex, blood pressure, blood cholesterol and smoking; all these are contributory causes of the disease. And yet people who publish papers are continually discovering others, so that the list of supplementary risk factors now stands at more than 300: for example, being an English speaker, not eating mackerel, not taking a siesta . . . The meaning of the term when it is used in so broad a way thus becomes rather debased: it hangs somewhere between 'association' and 'cause', and it is not clear in some commentaries exactly what position in this space it occupies. This is potentially confusing because the idea of 'cause' can be subtly insinuated by using the term in a particular way in a particular context. 'Not eating mackerel', etc., is not a cause of heart disease, and it is important to be clear that 'risk factor' must under no circumstances be allowed to mean 'cause'. In many ways it would be better to drop the term altogether, but it is now so well established that we have no choice but to live with it.

The importance of the new discoveries about stress, personality, the brain and the immune system, the relations between them and the implications of these for the health and longevity of the individual, cannot be overstated. They are crucial to the advancement of medicine, to the caring professions and to our general understanding of the nature of health and the person.

Chapter 1

BAD THINGS IN THE DIET.
SATURATED FATS AND CHOLESTEROL?

Medicine's greatest achievement this century has been the discovery of ways to prevent illness. More life has been saved, and its quality protected, through the isolation and proving of vaccines, and through the setting up of standards of hygiene, than through any advance in the treatment of illness once it has been correctly diagnosed.

But we are continually being told about new 'wonder drugs' and 'miracle cures' and no one can deny that the technology of modern medicine is truly impressive. So what justification is there for this opening statement?

In the treatment of people who are sick with today's illnesses, rarely, if ever, does a new wonder drug or miracle cure live up to its expectations. Early heart transplants were at first hailed with tremendous enthusiasm as a 'miraculously effective solution'; surgeons were lionised. But little attention was paid to the follow-up of the patients—the problems they suffered and their deaths. The same is true of so many new treatments. Only when the first flush of enthusiasm has evaporated and the facts quietly been gathered in is it realised that new procedures create problems of their own in the form of undesirable side-effects, and that many are in reality little better than placebos.

Great claims have been made for the treatment of cancer —by surgery, by radiation and by chemotherapy. But the voice of dissent from within medicine grows louder. Much of the research that has been done comparing treated people with untreated people is flawed. For example, the finding that people with breast cancer who are treated using surgery and radiation enjoy longer survival than those who are not treated, has been shown to be biased from the start: the people in the untreated group tend to have more advanced cancer when they first arrive at the hospital for examination.[1]

A 1985 editorial in the prestigious *New England Journal of Medicine*[2] concluded that, except for selected cases of stomach and breast cancer, chemotherapy, when used in conjunction with surgery, has produced no demonstrable improvement in the survival of patients with the ten most common cancers.

And even these cautions do not take into account the debased quality of life that a person having to undergo one of these treatments must endure. Against the power of preventive medicine, treatments of people who are already ill look rather clumsy and last-ditch.

Bacterial infections, especially tuberculosis, were until the 1930s the major causes of deaths in industrial countries —in young and middle-aged people as well as in the elderly. By the 1970s these infections had become preventable and treatable and were rarely the prime causes of death. Life expectancy was greatly improved. This was mainly due to the better health of children so that more of the population survived into middle and old age.

Today the principal causes of death are circulatory diseases, especially heart disease and strokes, and cancer. Diseases that affect all age groups equally have been more or less eliminated (leaving aside, for the moment, AIDS), and we are now most concerned about conditions that are related to age—the so-called chronic degenerative conditions through which the chance of dying increases dramatically as one grows older. Fig. 1 illustrates this pattern for deaths due to cancer.

Getting at the causes and prevention of chronic degenerative conditions has proved to be more difficult than with infections, where it is a matter of proving that a particular germ is the cause and then finding and purifying a vaccine that reinforces the defences of the immune system against

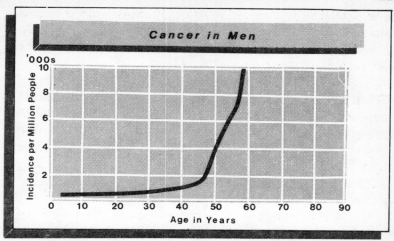

Fig. 1* An example of the sharp rise in degenerative and fatal illnesses with age.

*Source: Le Fanu, J. *Eat Your Heart Out*, 1987, London: Macmillan.

that germ. The scientific investigation of heart disease and cancer is not like this, partly because these conditions *are* related to age. Until we discover the genetic key to preventing the ageing process itself we have to accept that age is in a sense an unavoidable 'cause' of these conditions. But not everyone dies from heart disease or cancer, and of those who do, some live longer than others. So it has become appropriate in the case of age-related conditions to talk about 'premature' heart disease, 'early' cancer, etc., and to reason that even if it proves impossible to prevent the disease itself, we can identify individuals and populations in whom its appearance is untimely and then look for additional, perhaps more preventable, causes. These conditions, therefore, instead of being reckoned to have just one cause, are thought of as caused by a number of contributory factors, some of which may be capable of modification while others, like age, at least at the moment, are not.

A convention has grown up in medicine to refer to these multiple causes as 'risk factors'. Heart disease is widely believed to have five major risk factors: age, sex (it affects men more than women), blood pressure, smoking and blood cholesterol. Of these five the last three are things we may be able to change, the first two are not. Consequently, a huge programme of research has grown up to try and find ways of lowering blood pressure and blood cholesterol and encouraging people to stop smoking.

EPIDEMIOLOGY

How do we find out what the risk factors are for heart disease or for cancer? We can start by studying the prevalence of these diseases in different countries and in different communities. The proportion of the population dying of heart disease varies widely from country to country. Figures published by the World Health Organisation, for example, show that in 1980 deaths from heart disease were five times more common among American men than among Japanese men. Statistics like this are interesting and always lead to much speculation about why such a big difference should exist. It is not very useful just to say that 'being American' is a risk factor for heart disease—there is considerable variation among other countries; the Finns have an even higher rate than the Americans. Besides, studies of immigrants show that the incidence of heart disease in immigrant communities approximates to that of the country of residence rather than the country of origin. But the question of what differences exist between populations such as the Americans and the Japanese, which might account for such a large discrepancy in heart disease, understandably intrigues researchers and the search for an explanation goes on.

The branch of medicine concerned with revealing variations in the prevalence of a disease in different groups of people is known as *epidemiology*. The ultimate aim of epidemiology is to relate specific diseases to specific environmental causes by identifying the risk factors at work. In terms of funding, it is far and away the most fashionable of all medicine's sub-disciplines. Over the last 15 years numerous new specialist journals have emerged, while others have changed their names so as to modernise their image. The long established *Journal of Chronic Diseases* in 1988 changed its name to *Journal of Clinical Epidemiology*. The *Journal of Hygiene*, as it was before 1987, is now re-titled *Epidemiology and Infection*, and the old *British Journal of Preventive Medicine* has become the *Journal of Epidemiology and Community Heath*. A great deal of hope is pinned on the methods of this comparatively new subject.

There is some foundation for this optimism, for epidemiology's findings have proved of value in several areas of medicine. They have been able to define the effectiveness of vaccines and treatments for infectious diseases. They have helped assess the seriousness of work hazards, such as exposure to lead and other heavy metals and the risks associated with dusts such as asbestos. They have confirmed the clinically suspected relation between blood pressure and heart disease and between blood cholesterol level and heart disease. They have demonstrated a relation between smoking and both lung cancer and heart disease. They have confirmed the effectiveness of some forms of cancer screening. By providing descriptive statistics of incidence, and trends over a period of time, they have contributed to ante-natal health policy and to psychiatric care. Nevertheless, it cannot be claimed that epidemiology has ever on its own discovered the cause of any disease.

'Lies, damned lies, and statistics'

The purpose of epidemiology is to describe relationships and trends and thereby to help confirm or refute suspected relationships. Its data are neutral, descriptive statistics, and providing a study is properly carried out and the data properly collected, they represent straight statements of fact and as such cannot lie ('in 1980, deaths from coronary heart disease were five times more common among American men than among Japanese men' . . . etc.). The strength of this sort of data is in their neutrality and their dissociation from theories and ideas about causality. They cannot lie because as they stand they have no meaning.

The *interpretation* of these facts, however, is another story and one often besieged by controversy in the scientific community and inaccurate sensationalist reporting in the popular press. The Japanese are known to eat more fish and less fatty meat than the Americans. This fact has frequently been jumped on—and even sometimes simply assumed —as an explanation of why the Japanese have the lower rate of heart disease. But there are many other differences between the American and Japanese cultures, besides diet and the obvious genetic ones. The Japanese, for example, smoke more than the Americans but no one would want to suggest that smoking protects you from heart disease. There are differences in their respective diets besides consumption of meat and fish; equally important, there are profound differences in the history, environment and lifestyle of the peoples in the two countries.

Once an association is discovered between incidence of a particular disease and, say, some aspect of diet, it is very tempting to see one as the cause of the other. Medicine makes the headlines more than any other branch of science, and any suggestion that a particular food is healthy or unhealthy is guaranteed a high public profile. Epidemiological findings have a particular lure for aspiring journalists who are looking for a story with immediate appeal and with a practical message—'Eat more fish and less meat and you'll reduce your chances of heart disease!' . . . 'Change your diet and save your life!'.

Great care needs to be taken in the interpretation of epidemiological data, but very often it is not. The distinction between statistical associations, or correlations, and causes is a crucial one. The temptation to read associations as causes is widely succumbed to and can too easily result in public acceptance of 'truths' that are at best unproved and at worst incorrect. Sweeping statements of 'fact' are put forward with great confidence—for example: 'Saturated fats, which lead to blockages in the arteries, are a major underlying cause of heart disease . . . There is general agreement that there should be a big reduction in intake of saturated fats.' (*The Food Scandal*, by Caroline Walker and Geoffrey Cannon.)[3] 'General agreement' there may be, but it is quite unjustified by the facts, as I shall try to demonstrate in this chapter.

Epidemiology certainly has the power to *suggest* causes and effects. It *may* indeed be the case that eating less meat and more fish reduces your chances of getting heart disease, but this must be proved beyond simple comparisons between countries whose populations differ in so many ways. The only really convincing proof is a demonstration that by changing the diet of a group of people—for instance, by persuading them to eat more fish and less meat—the rate of heart disease in that group diminishes in proportion to the extent of the change in the diet. This acid test is known as an *intervention* study. Just such a test helped show without any doubt that smoking causes lung cancer. But it is surprising how few of the supposed facts about diet and health stand up to it.

The correlation between smoking and lung cancer is strong. The death rate from the disease is ten times higher among smokers than non-smokers—shown in more than 30 different studies. But even this, on its own, is not sufficient to conclude that smoking causes lung cancer. Without the crucial intervention study other possibilities exist—for example, there may be something in the genes or in the personalities of certain people that both makes them smoke and also predisposes them to lung cancer. Or perhaps lung cancer, long before it is diagnosed, itself inclines people to smoke. In either case, stopping smoking would be useless. But these and other possibilities were all discounted when it was shown that stopping smoking actually does reduce the risk and that the longer the time a person has stopped, the less the risk becomes. This proved definitively that smoking causes lung cancer.

The efforts that have been made to prove the diet-disease theory in the same way have turned out to be curiously unsuccessful. And there are other findings that present difficulties for the hypothesis and cast serious doubt on its validity, despite its widespread appeal. The most intensively researched and talked about aspect of diet and health is the relation between fat and cholesterol in the diet, cholesterol in the blood, and coronary heart disease. It is worth examining the evidence for this relation in some detail. Despite the huge publicity it has attracted, when we look at the evidence carefully, we see it to be confused and contradictory, and the conclusions that have been drawn from it unwarranted, often misleading and sometimes potentially dangerous.

Changing the diet to protect health offers a practical formula that is easy to follow and immediately accessible to everyone. So it is not altogether surprising to find popular magazines full of tips about the 'healthy diet' and about all the things we should avoid. Folk myths about what we should and shouldn't eat have been in circulation long before medicine and science. The scientific method is supposed to tell us which if any of these has any basis in fact. Original pieces of scientific research are first reported in professional journals. Such journals strive to maintain a high standard of scientific rigour. In order to do so research reports are somewhat technical in their style.

By the time the information in one of these reports reaches the public it has percolated down several levels of reporting. Original pieces of research are regurgitated in text books, review articles, and scientific journals with a wider readership, like *New Scientist*. From these sources they are picked up by the more serious journalists and broadcasters, and then again, by the tabloid press and popular media. It is easy to see how information culled from a scientific journal article, when it gets to the general public, is anything but first hand. No one except specialists wants to read the highly technical source material so the original is interpreted, simplified and condensed before it appears in front of the public. Given good, honest journalism, there is no reason why the public should not get a fair picture of what a particular piece of research showed. But the farther down the system information gets, because of the different professional interests of the people doing the reporting, the more the trend towards punchy, emotive headlines and away from strict adherence to the original message. News has a habit of taking over from fact.

Concern about possible effects of diet on health has led many governments to set up special committees made up of experts whose brief it is to publish guidelines on what constitutes a healthy diet. If the evidence about diet and disease was consistent and clear, we should expect these committees to have no trouble in reaching their conclusions. But agreement seems more difficult to achieve than it should be, both within a particular committee and between different ones. Conclusions are carefully qualified—for example, 'Coronary heart disease is a multifactorial disease, but diet is *probably* [my italics] one of the most important environmental factors' (*Diet, Nutrition and Health*— Report of the Board of Science and Education, March 1986—COMA (Committee On Medical Aspects of food policy)). A 1984 HMSO document, entitled *Diet, and Cardiovascular Disease*, states, 'Nine out of the ten members of the Panel have concluded individually that there is sufficient consistency in this evidence to make it more likely than not that the incidence of coronary heart disease will be reduced, or its age of onset delayed, by decreasing dietary intake of saturated fatty acids and total fat.'

These conclusions hardly resonate with confidence. In fact it has become something of a joke that agreement in these committees is typically reached on the basis of a show of hands rather than on clear scientific evidence.

Fact or fad?

Policy statements about what foods are good for you also have a disconcerting habit of changing with time. In the 1930s the message was very different from that of today: people were firmly encouraged to eat dairy products, especially milk, butter and eggs, to correct malnourishment and build the health of the nation. The Second World War saw severe rationing of dairy products and a diet high in carbohydrates, cereals and vegetables with no corresponding deterioration in the nation's health, yet the myth that dairy products were protective of health somehow persisted, even when the facts failed to support it.

By 1980, public opinion had completely reversed in the way that fashions do. What used to be regarded as the essentials for life were now almost taken for granted as the evil causes of high blood cholesterol and heart disease. Carbohydrates, until recently, were widely believed to be a major cause of obesity. But what are we to make of the report of the Board of Science and Education in March 1986 (COMA)?—'It is a common belief that one needs to limit the intake of all carbohydrates as a means of weight control. This runs counter to current (medical) thinking. It is therefore important that a key aim of nutritional education should be to counteract the results of decades of teaching aimed at reducing carbohydrate intakes.'

Old beliefs about diet were sincerely held at the time, by those advocating them and by the public. The question therefore must be asked whether today's 'facts' about diet are any more authentic than the dogmas of the past. Yes, they are backed by epidemiological findings, but we must remember that epidemiology only has the power to reveal associations, not causes. Looked at closely, the evidence for a 'healthy' diet, over and above a sufficient diet, is shot through with holes.

Fat, cholesterol and atherosclerosis

What indication is there that saturated fats—that is, fats of animal origin—and cholestrol in the diet cause premature heart disease?

The process of atherosclerosis is the gradual silting up of arteries due to deposits of fatty tissue. These deposits build up on the inside wall of the artery, rather like the furring of water pipes due to the slow deposit of chalk (Fig. 2).

This is a long process. It is likely that everyone to a greater or lesser extent undergoes it from childhood onwards. Large patches of fatty deposits, known as atheromatous plaques, or *atheroma*, can damage the lining of the artery by distorting it, by causing other particles in the blood to stick to their surface and by causing calcium to be deposited which makes the artery more brittle. The branches of coronary arteries, supplying the heart, are particularly susceptible because these represent points of maximum friction (Fig. 3).

Artherosclerosis only becomes dangerous when the build-up of deposits in an artery narrows the diameter of that artery sufficiently to impede or block the flow of blood. A heart attack, for example, may result from a blood clot (or thrombus) becoming trapped in the narrowed region of an artery so as to cut off the blood supply to the area beyond it, starving the heart of its supply of oxygen. Tiny particles in the blood, called platelets, are involved in the process of blood clotting. In the unhealthy artery they become stickier and have a tendency to clump together. The same sequence in one of the arteries supplying the brain results in a stroke.

Blood serum cholesterol

Cholesterol is a major ingredient of atheromatous plaques and it is known that the level of cholesterol in the blood-stream—or, more correctly, the blood *serum*—is a major

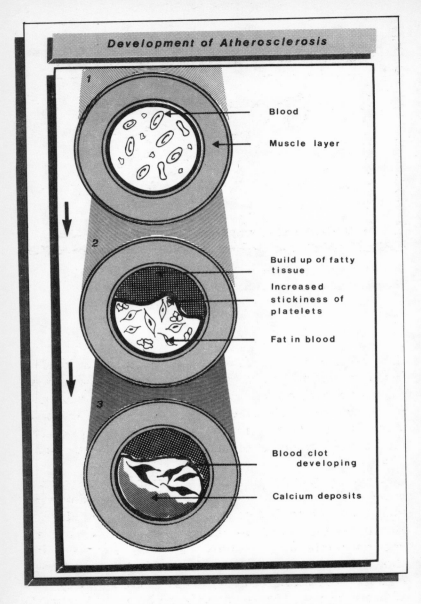

Fig. 2 Processes causing the main arteries gradually to become narrowed.

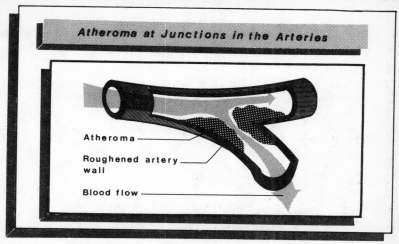

Atheroma at Junctions in the Arteries

Atheroma

Roughened artery wall

Blood flow

Fig. 3 Arterial junctions represent points of turbulence in the blood flow and so are particularly vulnerable.

risk factor for heart disease. The higher the level of blood, or serum, cholesterol, the greater the risk of heart disease. Serum cholesterol levels vary greatly from person to person. Data collected in the USA, for example, show that any level from 190 to 280 milligrams of cholesterol per 100 millilitres of blood can be considered normal (Fig. 4)

A tiny group of people suffer from an inherited condition known as *hypercholesteraemia*, which means they have very high levels of cholesterol in their blood. They develop atherosclerosis and heart disease early in life. The all-important intervention study has been done and has shown that reducing serum cholesterol in people with very high levels by means of drugs does indeed reduce the risk of heart disease. However, widespread use of drugs to lower serum cholesterol is undesirable since these drugs cause other problems.

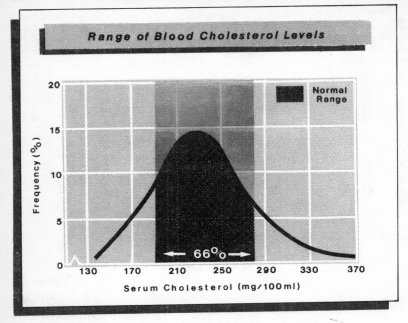

Fig. 4*   Blood serum cholesterol levels vary greatly among individuals. This graph is based on the American adult population. It is typical, and shows how wide the definition of 'normal' cholesterol is.

*Source: Brisson, G. J. *Lipids in Human Nutrition*. 1982, Lancaster: MTP Press.

A MYTH ABOUT CHOLESTEROL

It is very important to distinguish between serum cholesterol—cholesterol in the blood—and cholesterol in food. Cholesterol is essential to life. It is present in every cell in the body. It is a building block for many hormones and a vital component of cell membranes. The body—principally the liver—manufactures three to four times the amount of cholesterol that is eaten. So the picture painted by the less scrupulous media, of cholesterol as an evil, is a misinformed and misleading one.

Types of cholesterol

Certain forms of cholesterol appear to work against the formation of atheromatous plaques. Cholesterol is a fatty substance—a *lipid*—which on its own is insoluble in water. The body is a watery medium, and so cholesterol needs a special mechanism to carry it through the bloodstream. In effect, it requires an escort. These escorts are known as *lipoproteins*, and there are five types, classified according to their density and size:

VLDL	Very low density lipoproteins
LDL	Low density lipoproteins
IDL	Intermediate density lipoproteins
HDL	High density lipoproteins
VHDL	Very high density lipoproteins

For our purpose we need only distinguish two types, LDL and HDL. The 'density' in this system of labelling refers to the ratio of protein to fat, LDL having little protein and lots of fat, and HDL having little fat and lots of protein. HDL is the smaller and heavier of the two.

It is necessary to spell out these distinctions because HDL-cholesterol and LDL-cholesterol have very different effects in the blood. They are sometimes referred to, respectively, as 'good' and 'bad' cholesterol. LDL-cholesterol is the cholesterol we have been discussing up to now in this chapter. It carries cholesterol into tissues such as arteries and leaves it there, aiding and abetting atherosclerosis and heart disease. HDL, on the other hand, appears to remove it again and transport it to the liver for excretion and so is believed to play a benign, preventive role. Blood tests for cholesterol are usually expressed as a single score, *total cholesterol*, denoting the amount of cholesterol of whatever kind in the blood. But some doctors argue that the ratio of LDL-cholesterol to HDL-cholesterol is a better indication of an individual's risk of heart disease.

DIET AND SERUM CHOLESTEROL

We are now ready to address the fascinating question of whether what we eat affects the level of total or LDL-cholesterol in our blood and therefore our risk of developing heart disease. The conclusion of this chapter can be stated in anticipation: it is not what we eat that influences cholesterol in the blood to any significant extent, it is what the body does with ingested and self-made cholesterol. Internal regulating mechanisms are a much more powerful determinant of serum cholesterol, atherosclerosis and heart disease, than diet.

The evidence

The thesis that heart disease is influenced by diet, and that serum cholesterol level is the link, first arose from a classic series of experiments with animals carried out early this century. These showed that serum cholesterol levels in rabbits rose significantly when the rabbits were fed foodstuffs high in dietary cholesterol—meat, milk and eggs. But there is a problem with what to make of these experiments: rabbits are herbivores and the rabbit gut has not evolved so as to be able to cope with quantities of saturated fats and cholesterol such as are found in meat, milk and eggs. Today it is generally acknowledged that the human response to dietary fats and cholesterol is very different from that of most animals.

The evidence that extended the diet-heart thesis to humans was a major survey carried out in the 1950s by Ancel Keys.[4] Keys looked at seven countries where the incidence of heart disease varied from very low (Japan) to very high (Finland), the other countries being Greece, Yugoslavia, Italy, the United States and the Netherlands. Eleven thousand men took part in the study. Their blood pressure and serum cholesterol were measured, along with their dietary and smoking habits; they were then followed up for ten years and the incidence of heart disease in each of the seven countries was recorded. The study showed that the amount of saturated fat in the diet correlated both with the average level of serum cholesterol in each group and with the incidence of heart disease (Fig. 5).

These findings caused considerable excitement. They suggest that saturated fats in the diet are one of the culprits in the degenerative process leading to heart disease. But correlations are not causes and Keys' study only *suggests* and does not prove this. The seven countries studied are an odd mixture. The question had to be asked, how meaningful are comparisons between groups of people who are so different in so many respects?

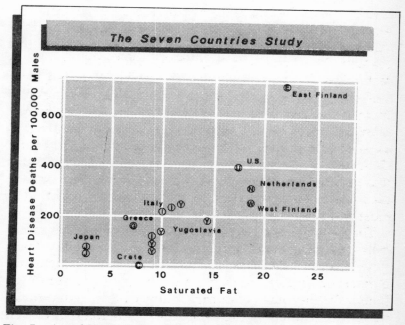

Fig. 5   Ancel Keys' Seven Countries Study based on various towns in Japan (J), Greece and Crete (G and C), Italy (I), Yugoslavia (Y), America (U), Netherlands (N) and Finland (F). Deaths from heart disease are shown according to estimated saturated fat in the diet.

Two approaches were taken to try to answer this: 1) look at some more countries, and 2) see if the relation between dietary fat and heart disease holds up among people of the same nationality.

1   When 20 countries are compared a much less clear pattern emerges, and when similar countries are compared the strong trend drawn in Fig. 5 disappears altogether and the diet-heart thesis runs into difficulties.[5] And there are other anomalies. The percentage of the diet taken as saturated fat is roughly the same in France as it is in Finland. Yet the Finns have five times the rate of heart disease of the French who, although they eat a lot of fat, have one of the lowest rates of heart disease in the world.

2   The relation between fat and heart disease that looked so compelling in Keys' original study has never been confirmed within a particular country. Some studies have found serum LDL-cholesterol to be lower in vegetarians than in meat eaters, but the findings of such studies do not show good agreement. It must be borne in mind that the habits and lifestyles of vegetarians typically differ from those of meat eaters in other ways besides diet; for example, perhaps vegetarians tend to smoke less and take more exercise.

A recent study of three English towns—Ipswich, Stoke-on-Trent and Wakefield—suggests that differences in diet, and in particular, in consumption of fat, is not a cause of differences in deaths from heart disease between one part of Britain and another.[6] The town with the highest rate of death from heart disease (Wakefield) recorded the lowest consumption of fat. Again, this relation should not be interpreted as causal, but it offers no support to the idea that diet affects heart disease.

Migrant studies
The second major line of evidence used to support the diet-heart thesis comes from studies of migrants. These

studies showed that people who move from a country with a low fat diet and a low rate of heart disease, such as Japan, to a country with a high fat diet and a high rate of heart disease, such as America, take on the pattern of disease that exists in the adopted country. So, Americanised Japanese consistently have a raised risk of heart disease.[7] It is widely assumed that changes in diet are responsible for this.

Diet, however, is only one of many environmental changes immigrants face, and here again, while studies of immigrants may *suggest* that changes in diet are responsible for changes in health patterns, they do not prove it. Again, on a closer look at these studies of immigrants we find that the diet-heart thesis runs into problems. The diet of Swedish and American people is said to be similar in terms of fat intake but the Swedes have the lower rate of heart disease. When Swedish people settle in America their rate of heart disease increases to that of indigenous Americans despite the fact that their diet has not changed much.[8] One piece of research showed that Japanese people moving to America and eating the high fat American diet but carrying on Japanese traditions in local communities, had a lower rate of heart disease than Japanese people there eating a Japanese diet.[9] These facts hint that something other than diet may be responsible for the changes in the health of immigrants.

The tendency for immigrants to substitute the patterns of disease of their adopted country for those of their native country seems to hold true for all diseases. The rate of heart disease among the majority of Japanese settling in America rises to the higher American rate. But the rate of strokes and cancer falls to the lower American rate. An environmental force of some nature is clearly at work here, but diet is not the only candidate and there are clues to suggest it may not be the right one.

Studies of Seventh Day Adventists
Much has been made of the observation that Seventh Day

Adventists, who are vegetarians, have a lower rate of heart disease than the general population. But Adventists are a group with many other peculiar characteristics besides diet. Mormons, another highly religious sectarian group, but eaters of meat and dairy products, also have a low rate of heart disease.[10] Again, something other than food seems responsible for these differences.

Trends over time

Death certificate records allow us to plot changes in death rate from a particular disease, or set of diseases, over a period of time. Fig. 6, taken from data published by the World Health Organisation, shows trends in deaths from coronary disease for five countries (chosen for their contrasts) over the period 1968 to 1982.

The graph shows at a glance the big variation between different countries. It also shows some significant trends over time. The rate for American males, which had been climbing until 1968, was seen to fall dramatically throughout the subsequent 15 years. This is often attributed to greater health consciousness, although the American diet itself did not change much throughout these years. These trends, interesting as they are, are very difficult to interpret. There were major developments in coronary care resuscitation and in coronary artery by-pass surgery during this time. And this is the period when beta-blockers, a group of drugs that can reduce high blood pressure—one of the main risk factors for heart disease—came into more general use. A study of several thousand residents of Alameda County, in California, indicated that none of the traditional risk factors—blood pressure, serum cholesterol, etc.—could account for the decline in American heart deaths from 1965 to 1974.[11] The drop was accompanied by an increase in the use of medical services, especially among young people. So maybe this trend is simply due to people taking advantage of an improvement in medical care.

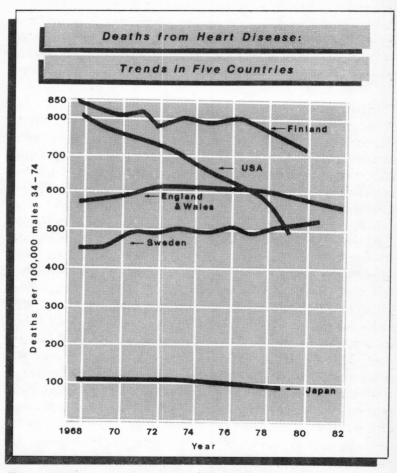

Fig. 6 The variations between countries in deaths due to coronary heart disease (c.h.d.). This assumes that c.h.d. is being diagnosed in the same way by doctors in the different countries.

The data available for food consumption in these countries over these years is thin and of questionable reliability. Typically, no distinction is made between saturated and polyunsaturated fat. What data there are provide little support for the diet-heart thesis. In Japan, where the rate of heart disease has always been low, rates continue to fall in spite of a growing taste for Western foods and a big increase in saturated fat consumption.

The Second World War saw rationing and a universal and radical change in the British diet. Fat and sugar consumption fell sharply and fibre consumption rose. Many commentators have claimed, along with the Registrar General in 1949, that the death rate from heart disease fell, or slowed down, during the years of rationing. However, in 1940, an alteration was made in the conventions for coding cause of death in cases where more than one cause of death was recorded on a death certificate. This had the effect of fewer deaths being attributed to heart disease under the new convention than there would have been under the old one. When the wartime data are re-examined and corrected for this artefact of method the following conclusion is reached: 'After allowance for changes in the rules for coding cause of death, and for the sharp increase in all-cause mortality in 1940, there is little to suggest that time trends in coronary heart disease were much influenced by the war.'[12]

The boom in health foods, the popularity of vegetarian food and the vast number of published books and articles on the subject leave little doubt that the British public have grown more concerned with healthy eating over the last 15 years. On the diet-heart thesis, these supposedly healthier foods ought to result in lower serum cholesterol levels. Has the cholesterol level of the British people fallen over this time?

A report in 1988 in the *British Medical Journal* from Jim Mann and his team bears directly on this question.[13] Serum cholesterol levels were sampled in 12,092 men and women from four British towns, Glasgow, Leicester, London and

Oxford. Levels were compared with those measured in a similar study back in 1974. Cholesterol levels were virtually unchanged. The authors attribute this to the failure of health education to persuade the public to change its lifestyle. But could not the finding that cholesterol levels are unchanged be better explained on the grounds that diet has little influence on cholesterol in the blood?

INTERVENTION STUDIES

We now turn to the most important line of evidence on the diet-heart thesis. If saturated fats and cholesterol in the diet influence serum cholesterol and the incidence of heart disease, it must be possible to demonstrate that by intervening and improving people's diets, their cholesterol levels can be lowered and their rate of heart disease reduced.

1   Small-scale studies

Several studies have been done in which a group of individuals, such as patients in a hospital ward, are assigned to different dietary regimes, and changes in their blood cholesterol measured. Unfortunately, this group of studies presents us with contradictory messages and no consensus has emerged from it. Many have used as subjects people at risk for coronary heart disease—either because they have very high blood pressure or because they have an abnormally high level of serum cholesterol. Some do show that extreme modification to the diet can bring about a small reduction in blood cholesterol level, but this does not always last.

In a recent study by Jacqueline Edington and her colleagues,[14] 168 healthy volunteers on a low fat diet ate either two or seven eggs a week (eggs are extremely rich in cholesterol) for a 16-week experimental period. A small but significant increase in serum cholesterol was seen after four weeks in the group eating seven eggs compared with that in the group eating two eggs, but this was no longer apparent after eight weeks. This finding is interesting because it suggests a homeostatic, or regulating, influence at work, setting its own internal standard for cholesterol in the blood, which compensates for, and is relatively independent of, changes in the diet. Bearing in mind the essential functions of cholesterol in the healthy working of the body, and the fact that the body manufactures far more cholesterol than is present in the diet, a compensating mechanism of this nature makes sense. Perhaps what we are seeing in the eggs study is an adaptation of the body's own cholesterol production in response to raised levels in the diet.

Some findings are nothing short of embarrassing for the diet-heart lobby. By all accounts milk, which contains saturated fat and cholesterol, ought to raise the level of LDL-cholesterol in the blood. But one study,[15] that had volunteers drinking four pints of milk a day for two weeks, found blood samples taken before and after this experimental period revealed a significant fall in serum LDL-cholesterol.

Another experiment recently published in the *New England Journal of Medicine* must also be mentioned.[16] This clearly showed that stearic acid—a saturated fatty acid and one of the main constituents of beef fat— had the effect of *lowering* serum total cholesterol and serum LDL-cholesterol!

Overall, this group of studies does not support the diet-heart thesis. A few experiments have demonstrated very small changes in serum cholesterol attributable to very large variations in diet, mainly in groups of people with abnormally high serum cholesterol levels. So we can conclude that extreme variations in diet *can* cause changes in cholesterol in the blood, but they do so unreliably and the changes are too small to be of concern to the general population: they are insignificant against the wide variation among healthy people in blood cholesterol level. Moreover, these changes are often only temporary, presumably on account of the body's setting of its own standard.

2 Large scale studies

The final experiments to consider are known as the Primary Prevention Studies. These were set up in the 1970s to see if an intensive programme of intervention, in the form of advice, counselling and propaganda, could be effective in reducing the risk of heart disease in very large groups of people. None of them represents a direct test of the diet-heart thesis because the interventions were of the 'shotgun' type and included pressure to stop smoking and to take more exercise as well as encouragement to eat less saturated fat. Three of the studies used drugs as well to treat high risk individuals. Nevertheless, they are the most expensive and extensive experiments in the history of medicine and their findings are interesting.

The design of all six studies is similar. Each took a large sample of people, divided them into two or more matched groups, then 'treated' one group but left the other group alone (the comparison, or 'control' group). Everyone was followed up for about ten years and it was hoped to be able to show that the incidence of heart disease and death due to heart disease during this ten-year period had been lower in the intervention group than in the control group. The studies are summarised in Table 1.

Of the six trials, only two interventions—those in the LRCCPPT (Lipid Research Clinics Coronary Primary Prevention Trial) and the Oslo studies—resulted in a reduction in rate of heart disease in the treated group relative to the control group. Both these used as subjects men known to be at risk for heart disease due to a high level of blood cholesterol, and since the LRCCPPT trial used the cholesterol-lowering drug, cholestyramine, as part of the intervention procedure, this one was not primarily a study of environmental or lifestyle factors at all. In the large World Health Organisation Study, which involved some

TABLE 1
The Primary Prevention Studies

Study	Sample	Intervention
Multiple Risk Factor Intervention Trial (MRFIT—USA)[17]	12,000 middle-aged men with normal serum cholesterol.	Counselling to stop smoking and reduce fat in diet. Drug treatment for hypertensives.
World Health Organisation (WHO—Europe)[18]	60,881 middle-aged men with normal serum cholesterol.	Advice on a cholesterol-lowering diet, control of smoking, over-weight, blood pressure and exercise.
The Oslo Study in Norway[19]	16,202 middle-aged men with high serum cholesterol.	Counselling to stop smoking, advice about diet and overweight.
Lipids Research Clinics—Coronary Primary Prevention (LRCCPPT—USA)[20]	3,806 middle-aged men with high serum cholesterol.	Cholesterol reducing drug plus dietary changes.
The North Karelia Study in Finland[21]	10,000 men and women from the general population.	Community intervention programme, with advice on smoking, diet, exercise and proper use of health services and rehabilitation facilities.
The Göteborg Study in Sweden[22]	30,000 men with normal serum cholesterol.	Drug treatment for some hypertensives and men with high serum cholesterol. Anti-smoking education. Dietary advice.

60,000 middle-aged men employed in 80 factories in Belgium, Italy, Poland and the United Kingdom, the intervention programme did have some effect—heart disease was down about ten per cent in the group receiving advice. This difference, although it was not technically significant, does perhaps carry some implications for public health policy. Just what these implications are, however, is hard to say. As a scientific test of the diet-heart thesis we are still left in the dark. The study tells us very little because we do not know which one of the modified risk factors, or which combination of them, was responsible for the reduction in rate of heart disease. The whole effect may have been due to advice to take more exercise, or to cut down smoking.

The results of these massive trials are generally reckoned to be disappointing. The most important thing to note is that in *none* of them did the intervention effort result in a reduction in overall mortality—that is, deaths from all causes including heart disease; not even in the LRCCPPT trial, in which a drug was used. In every trial the survival of those people who were the target of the supposedly health-promoting package was more or less the same as that of the comparison group who were left alone to mind their own business.

THE DESIRABILITY OF LOWERING SERUM CHOLESTEROL

The studies reviewed in this chapter make it clear that the relation between diet and serum cholesterol is tenuous. It has proved extremely difficult to bring about even small changes in serum cholesterol other than in people with dangerously high levels. Even when drugs are used to reduce cholesterol in the blood their effectiveness tends to diminish over time. The body seems intent on setting its own level and keeping it there.

But aside from the possibility of lowering serum cholesterol the Primary Prevention Studies raise the issue of the desirability of doing so. In those instances where blood cholesterol levels were reduced, through advice about lifestyle or by giving drugs, so that the risk of heart disease declined, overall mortality—deaths from all causes —was unchanged. Is interfering in people's lives so as to try to force down their levels of blood cholesterol perhaps based on too simplistic a version of how the body works?

If lowering serum cholesterol reduces heart disease but not overall mortality, what other effects is it having? Is there any independent evidence linking low cholesterol with raised risk of non-coronary diseases? Fourteen studies (one involving 39,000 men and women) have reported an inverse relation between serum cholesterol and cancer of all kinds—that is, the lower the level of cholesterol in the blood, the greater the risk of cancer. However, a further eight studies found no such association and one found a positive association for colorectal cancer.[23-25] This evidence suggesting a link between low serum cholesterol and non-coronary diseases is mixed and calls for caution in its interpretation. Nevertheless, the weight of evidence, especially recent studies using large numbers of people, suggests that something is there to be explained.

Cancer can upset the body's caloric balance and can itself cause a fall in serum cholesterol. This fact is often used to explain the association. But a cancer would have to be fairly well advanced and its presence almost certainly self-evident before this could happen.

To find out if the association between low blood cholesterol and cancer is genuine, a research team in Maryland, USA, set up a big study of 12,488 healthy American men and women whose serum cholesterol was measured in the early 1970s and who were all checked for diagnosis of cancer about six years later. Initial serum cholesterol levels were divided into five categories, or quintiles, from low to high. The results showed men and women in the lowest quintile to have twice the risk of dying from cancer as those in the highest quintile.[23]

To rule out the possibility that cancer had itself caused low blood cholesterol, the authors analysed the relation between blood cholesterol and cancer according to the interval between cholesterol measurement and cancer diagnosis. If cancers were lowering serum cholesterol, we would expect this relation to be strongest the shorter the interval. In fact the opposite was found. The relation was strongest for cancers diagnosed six years or more after blood cholesterol was measured. This goes against any explanation of the findings on the grounds that cancer had caused lower levels of serum cholesterol.

A similar study of 15,000 Scottish men and women, followed up for 12 years, was very recently reported in the *British Medical Journal*.[24] This showed the expected strong association between high levels of cholesterol in the blood and deaths from heart disease. But here again, deaths in general were not related to serum cholesterol. And in this study too, the absence of a relation between blood cholesterol and overall mortality was due to people with low levels of cholesterol dying more frequently from other causes; in the case of men, cancer. The 'preclinical hypothesis'—the possibility that cancer had caused low cholesterol—was again discounted by the fact that the relation held up for more than four years after the original blood samples had been taken.

With their large numbers and strongly significant findings, the Maryland and the Scottish studies, together with a Finnish study of 39,000 men and women,[25] must be taken seriously. They do not prove that a low level of blood cholesterol causes cancer and other illnesses, but this certainly must be entertained as a hypothesis. Cholesterol is an essential component of cell membranes. Some authors have speculated that lowering serum cholesterol may interfere with the surface structure of cells and their replication. In one study, a cholesterol-lowering drug was shown to increase mortality from cancer.[26] In another study, of women over the age of 60, death rates from all causes, including heart disease, were highest at the lowest levels of serum cholesterol.[27] Whatever the findings of these studies eventually turn out to mean, they stand as warnings against the wisdom of any blanket policy to reduce serum cholesterol levels in the population at large.

CONCLUSION

The evidence presented in this chapter is sufficient to demonstrate two things:

1 Serum total and LDL-cholesterol ('bad cholesterol') are very resistant to change through a modified diet. Extreme modifications in diet cause changes that are inclined to revert over time.

2 A diet low in saturated fat and cholesterol to reduce blood serum cholesterol may be relevant to people with pathologically high levels of serum cholesterol, but has no application as a universal panacea. There is even a danger that extreme diets may lower serum cholesterol in some individuals so that the risk of other illnesses, such as cancer, is raised.

There can be no doubt that recommendations about saturated fats and cholesterol in the diet, and about their effect on cholesterol in the blood and heart disease, have been far too eager. Too much has been said based on too premature an interpretation, and often a misinterpretation, of the facts. Proclaiming, declaiming and denouncing have for some reason, perhaps political, perhaps commercial, taken over from reasoned reporting and have led to a serious misleading of the public.

On the matter of whether we should adopt the general attitude that lower serum cholesterol levels are healthy, an editorial in the *Lancet*, June 24th 1989, has this to say: 'Even supposing that people wish to lower their cholesterol without any awareness of whether it is high or low, might not some people already in a low range be exposed to increased risk of cancer?'

A. E. Dugdale, in a letter to the *Lancet*, calculates that if we use drugs or extreme diets to reduce serum cholesterol in the general population by ten per cent (itself no easy matter), this would prolong life by an average of one year, and in those with abnormally high blood cholesterol, about three years. But the main result would be an increase in deaths from other causes, especially cancer. 'The main result for the health services would be a transfer of case loads and resources from cardiac to cancer units . . . We all die, and, at the cost of one year, heart disease may be preferable to cancer.'[28]

Chapter 2

ANOTHER BAD THING IN THE DIET AND SOME GOOD THINGS?

DIETARY FAT AND CANCER

Not only has saturated fat in the diet been indicted as a major cause of atherosclerosis, it is believed by some authors also to be a prime contributor to certain forms of cancer. Why saturated fat should be the constant villain in all this is something of a mystery. Perhaps it is because these fats carry so many pleasant flavours. The argument about fat and cancer runs along lines parallel to that about heart disease. First, there is a strong correlation between the average consumption of saturated fat in different countries and the corresponding mortality from certain cancers, notably breast and bowel cancer. Second, studies again show that these forms of cancer have increased among Japanese immigrants to the United States, paralleled by an increase in consumption of saturated fats from the low Japanese standard to the characteristically high American one.

The same flaws in the argument are repeated for fat and cancer as were evident for fat and heart disease. As facts, the differences between countries, and between immigrants and non-immigrants, are unchallengeable. As evidence of causes and effects they are not sufficient. The close correspondence between fat intake and breast cancer tells us only that breast cancer is more common in developed countries, where consumption of saturated fats is highest. But we know that the risk of breast cancer increases the earlier menstruation starts, the greater the age at first pregnancy and the longer the use of oral contraceptives.[1] And we know that all three of these factors correlate closely with the degree of industrialisation and affluence of a country. Any one of them offers a plausible alternative to the theory that fat causes cancer.

It is interesting to note that when Japanese people move to America the rates of those cancers that are more common in Japan (cancers of the stomach and of the oesophagous) *decline* to the lower American rate.[2] It would be wrong to say that a change in saturated fat consumption is responsible for this decline, any more than to say it is the cause of the increase in breast cancer. We must remember, it is not only diet that changes for a Japanese man or woman settling in America.

When we look at studies of individuals within a particular country, the same confused and contrary set of findings is found as when heart disease is the object of study. None of these studies confirms the strong relationship between saturated fat and breast or bowel cancer, suggested by comparisons between different countries. And no convincing evidence comes from the most testing of these—prospective studies, in which the aim is to predict rates of cancer from dietary data; even from one study of more than 90,000 Californian women.[3] There are no intervention studies of diet and cancer comparable to those for diet and heart disease.

The research team at the University of Maryland have pointed out that in the United States between 1910 and 1970, the death rate from breast cancer rose while saturated fat consumption stayed more or less constant. There was, however, a strong correlation between the increase in breast cancer and the consumption of vegetable fats, which tripled, throughout this period.[4] There is again no reason to conclude that vegetable fats cause breast cancer, but it does suggest that something other than saturated fats may be the culprit.

The diet-cancer thesis, like the diet-heart thesis, when scrutinised more closely, fails to hold up. Here is the conclusion reached by a reviewer of the evidence: 'Despite the encouraging pointers from descriptive epidemiology of intriguing world-wide variations and changes in certain migrant groups, this evidence largely reduces to over-nutrition, alcohol and a lack of vegetables and fruit.' (Kinlen, L. K. in *Food and Health*, ed. R. Cottrell, 1987.)

In this chapter we shall consider another villain in the public eye—salt—and also some fairy godmothers—aspects of the diet that are supposed to be especially desirable because they protect health.

SALT AND ESSENTIAL HYPERTENSION

'Essential hypertension' means high blood pressure which is not the result of a recognised cause, the most common one being kidney disease. The word 'essential' is medical jargon for 'cause unknown'. Blood pressure is expressed as a fraction: *systolic* pressure (the pressure in the arteries when the heart contracts) over *diastolic* pressure (the press-ure in the arteries when the heart is relaxed). By conven-tion, the numbers in the fraction denote the height in millimetres of a column of mercury. As is the case for blood cholesterol, the variation in blood pressure between people is considerable, and there is a certain variation in the individual's blood pressure at different times. The World Health Organisation has defined the 'normal' range as a systolic pressure of between 100 and 140 mm, and a dias-tolic pressure of between 60 and 90 mm. Fig. 7 gives some idea of the wide range of blood pressure levels between individuals. The average, or absolutely normal, level is 120/80. Hypertension is defined as a blood pressure of 160/95 or more.

Blood pressure is an extremely important index as it is one of the major risk factors for heart disease, along with serum cholesterol and smoking. Even a modest rise in blood pressure above the normal range is associated with an increased chance of dying early. High blood pressure puts a strain on the heart and exaggerates wear and tear on

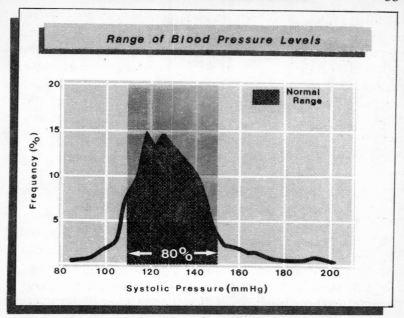

Fig. 7*   Blood pressure levels, like the levels of serum cholesterol, vary considerably from person to person. This graph is concerned with systolic pressure, but diastolic pressure shows a similar pattern. Note again how wide the 'normal' range is.

*Source: modified from Rushmer, R. F. *Cardiovascular Dynamics*, 1961, 2nd ed., Philadelphia: Saunders.

arteries, causing them to become more brittle. It accelerates atherosclerosis, which in turn raises blood pressure. In this way a vicious circle is set up (Fig. 8).

It is also one of medicine's most useful measures because it is so easy to obtain. As anyone who has had to go to hospital knows, the first tests done as standard procedures are those for temperature and blood pressure.

In most, but not quite all, societies blood pressure is found to increase with age. This is so in all the developed countries where high blood pressure is not uncommon. In

Britain about a fifth of the population over the age of 40 has high blood pressure.

Given these facts, it is not surprising that doctors and researchers are very keen to find ways of treating and preventing essential hypertension. Drug treatment is one method. Drugs known as beta-blockers, acting on the brain and nervous system, are effective in lowering blood pressure and have been in use since the 1950s. New varieties are continually being made.

However, a major study carried out by the Medical Research Council and reported in 1985[5] indicates that to treat people with these drugs routinely, unless they have suffered a heart attack or are severely hypertensive, is ill-advised. In this study, 17,354 men and women with mild hypertension were given blood pressure lowering drugs

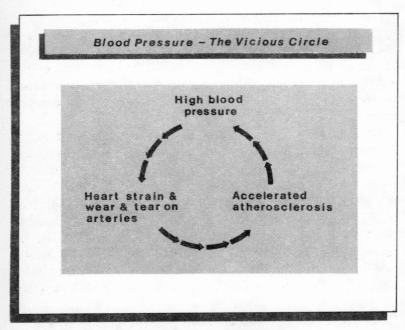

Fig. 8 How high blood pressure can lead on to atherosclerosis.

and watched for an average of five years. While the incidence of strokes was reduced in those given the drugs, that of heart disease and overall mortality was unaffected.

Risk factors for essential hypertension

A host of things have been proposed as risk factors for essential hypertension. Leaving aside those we can do nothing about, such as age, race and family history, the potentially modifiable ones that have been suggested are: heavy drinking, smoking, obesity, lack of exercise, lack of sleep, lack of calcium, psychological stress and, of course, diet. It has to be underlined that each one of these is no more than a hotly debated *possibility*. It is not difficult to imagine the many complex inter-relations there might be among them. Do heavy drinkers perhaps also tend to smoke and eat poorer diets? Do people drink, smoke and lose sleep when they are stressed? Etc. The intriguing issue of psychological stress will be dealt with in the subsequent chapters of this book. For the moment we resume the strangely elusive search for villains in the diet, with a look at what actually has been discovered in relation to another popular myth—that salt raises blood pressure and so is bad for you.

Obviously, a tremendous quantity of salt, just like a tremendous quantity of anything, is harmful. Among the Chinese, eating a cupful of salt was once a method of committing suicide. But a modest amount of salt in the diet is palatable and some salt is essential. In Nigeria, salt was traded by trans-Saharan Berbers as a precious commodity until transport become mechanised and routes to the interior were opened up. Rumour has it that salt traded pound for pound with gold. This is probably not true but it illustrates the value put on salt when it is in scarce supply.

Does salt in the diet affect blood pressure?

The theories and arguments that dietary salt influences blood pressure levels show a remarkable symmetry to those put forward in relation to saturated fat and heart disease. The same incautious reasoning prevails. Cross-cultural comparisons reveal that hypertension is rare among the few surviving primitive cultures scattered around the world, and the tendency for blood pressure to increase with age, seen so reliably in the developed world, appears to be absent in these communities. Studies by anthropologists have clearly shown that when a primitive culture is 'developed' and assimilated into the industrial world, the healthy pattern of a low, stable blood pressure is broken and blood pressures start to rise, sometimes quite dramatically, and continue to do so with advancing age.[6]

Changes forced on primitive cultures are profound and wide-ranging; consuming more salt is just one of many typical dietary changes. And there are numerous other changes and upheavals, apart from diet. To single out salt as the culprit in all this is to force the issue beyond reasonable limits. Industrialised communities are more affluent and the people in them generally eat more of everything than their primitive counterparts. Obesity is much more common, and patterns of physical activity and exercise change. Some authors have suggested that the stress of social disruption itself might be responsible. Perhaps something important is lost when the rituals and bonds that characterise close-knit primitive communities are disrupted and traditions disappear. We shall return to this idea later in the book.

Certain anthropological observations run counter to the salt-hypertension thesis. The blood pressure of a secluded group of Italian nuns who eat a diet high in salt has remained normal for 20 years, while that of women in a nearby village has risen sharply over this time.[7] In Malawi, a country undergoing rapid economic change, but where salt consumption remains low, blood pressures of rural and urban adults are nevertheless rising fast.[8] These two counter-instances suggest salt may not be the primary culprit and that maybe we should be casting the net rather wider in the search for the cause of raised blood pressure in these situations. A reviewer of this area of study ends with this conclusion: 'The evidence that it is the absence of salt in the diets of primitive tribes which keeps blood pressure low is poor and the case is overstated. Changes in acculturation and other nutrients may be equally or more important.' (Heagerty, A. M. In *Food and Health*, ed. R. Cottrell, 1987.)

INTERVENTION STUDIES: EXPERIMENTS LIMITING AND ENRICHING SALT IN THE DIET

A large number of experiments have been designed and carried out to test the salt-hypertension thesis by seeing what happens to blood pressure when people are on a low or a high salt diet. Some of these are genuine intervention studies: a group of subjects is fed a low (or high) salt diet and the average blood pressure in this group is compared with that in a comparison group of subjects given normal diets. In almost all these experiments the subjects are hypertensives—patients known to have raised blood pressure. Some do indeed show significant effects on blood pressure due to changes in the salt content of the diet, but reducing salt in the diet also reduces fluid retention and thus body weight. Many authors believe this weight loss may entirely account for the positive findings. It is interesting that in experiments where salt restriction is moderate and is not accompanied by any fluid loss, no effect on blood pressure is seen.[9]

However, for every experiment showing a beneficial effect of salt-reduction on blood pressure there is at least one showing no such effect, and few researchers have been able to correlate salt intake with individual blood pressure levels. Reactions to changes in dietary salt are unpredictable and occasionally, in some individuals, salt reduction is accompanied by a *rise* in blood pressure.[10]

Eighty years of this research does not provide good support for the salt-hypertension thesis. The conclusion must be that extreme restriction in dietary salt *can* lower blood pressure in hypertensive people under some (as yet ill-defined) conditions. But blood pressure, like blood cholesterol, appears extremely resistant to change, especially in those who fall within the normal range. In one study in which a group of people were fed highly salt-enriched diets, it took a 30-fold increase in salt intake to bring about an increase in systolic blood pressure of 1.4 per cent, and an 80-fold increase to cause a rise of 8.3 per cent![11] These variations bear little resemblance either to variations in diet in the real world or to variations between individuals in blood pressure levels.

A study of more than 10,000 men and women, randomly sampled in 52 centres around the world, has recently been completed. It is known as the *Intersalt Study*,[12] and its aim was to look at the relation between salt excretion in the urine and blood pressure level. A weak but significant association was found. Calculations were made about the effect that cutting our salt consumption would have on blood pressure if this was taken on board as general policy. A substantial reduction in dietary salt would result in the lowering of systolic pressure by 2.2 mm and diastolic pressure by 0.1 mm. Against the wide individual variation in blood pressure (Fig. 7, p. 53), these figures are trivial.

The conclusion we are drawn to is in every respect identical to that reached in connection with saturated fat and serum cholesterol. It is possible but extremely difficult to force a change in a person's blood pressure by altering the amount of salt in the diet. The body's internal regulating mechanisms are a much more powerful determinant of levels than even quite gross variations in the diet.

And, just as with cholesterol, the body seems to resent any attempt to interfere with its own settings. Fig. 9 nicely illustrates this. The graph is directly reproduced from a small intervention study in which a group of people were placed on a salt-restricted diet for a period of eight weeks. Sure enough, blood pressure responds to a low salt diet and

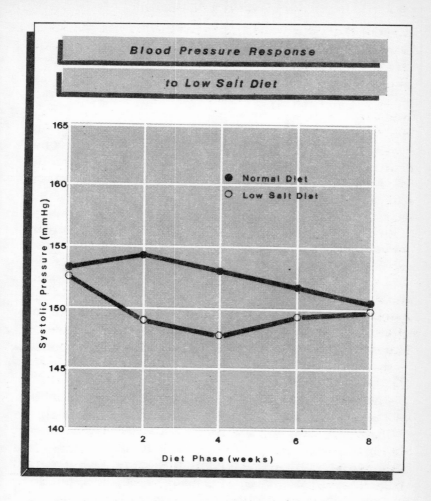

Blood Pressure Response to Low Salt Diet

Fig. 9* The authors of this experiment claim it shows that a low salt diet reduces systolic blood pressure. It does so for a while, but after eight weeks it no longer has any effect. This is a perfect illustration of how the body sets its own standards and resists 'help' from outside.

*Source: Australian National Health and Medical Research Council Dietary Salt Study Management Committee. Fall in blood pressure with moderate reduction in salt intake in mild hypertension. *Lancet*, 1989(1).

is significantly down after four weeks. But then it bounces back up again and at eight weeks is no different from that in the control group who are kept on an ordinary diet.[13]

SOME GOOD THINGS?

So far we have looked at three constituents of the normal diet—saturated fat, cholesterol and salt—which have come in for a huge amount of negative publicity over recent years. There can be no question that this has been overdone and fundamentally ill-informed. Premature conclusions have been drawn and inappropriate recommendations made—sometimes even by authoritative government committees.

Nearly as much energy has gone into telling us what we *should* eat. Where there are villains there must be heroes, and in the eyes of the popular media there is no shortage of these. But is the idea of health foods, over and above the ideal of an adequate, varied and not excessive diet, any more valid than the idea of foods that are bad for you?

Dietary fibre
Fibre is a complex carbohydrate present in plants, roots and cereals. Its important property is that it is not digested by the enzymes of the gut. The common practice in developed countries of processing and refining foods changes the carbohydrate content of many products by removing much of the fibre. The argument was made in the 1960s that this makes foods less natural and less healthy.

The thesis that fibre is good for you was originally based on the observations of two British doctors, Dennis Burkitt and Hugh Trowell, who had worked for many years in rural Africa. They noticed that atherosclerosis and certain diseases of the gut, including chronic constipation and cancer of the colon, are rare in rural Africans who eat a poorer diet—one much higher in fibre—than people living in Western cities.

Their observations attracted a lot of publicity. However, the obvious point was soon put that the average rural African differs from the average Westerner in many ways, two important ones being physical activity and exposure to sunlight. Much later, in 1985, the *Lancet* carried a report showing that mortality from cancer of the colon in the United States is highest in people exposed to the least amount of natural sunlight. The care that is so essential in interpreting comparisons between cultures was again, unfortunately, not taken, any more than it was with regard to fat and salt. Once more, in the absence of proper scientific back-up, the temptation to read causes into correlations has proved too much for many writers on the subject.

Trends over time have also led authors to false conclusions. Fig. 10 shows that an increase in fibre intake is associated with a reduction in cancer of the colon. But look at Fig. 11: this suggests that for a similar increase in fibre intake there is a corresponding increase in cancer of the stomach. If the graph in Fig. 10 is to be read as showing a causal relation, then why not the graph in Fig. 11? In which case all a fibre-supplemented diet will achieve is to exchange one form of cancer for another. The point is of course that, tempting as it may be, without other evidence, *neither* of these trends is to be taken as showing a cause and effect.[14]

It is not difficult to carry out an experimental test of the fibre hypothesis using some form of intervention. A group of patients or healthy people is fed a fibre-supplemented diet, while a comparable control group remains on a normal diet and any improvement in symptoms is recorded. The results of such studies show that a beneficial effect on symptoms can be obtained by supplementing the diet with fibre for some diseases of the gut—notably irritable bowel syndrome. However, these diseases characteristically respond to placebos (treatments that work purely through suggestion), and when the effect of the fibre supplement is compared to the effect of a placebo, there is typically no

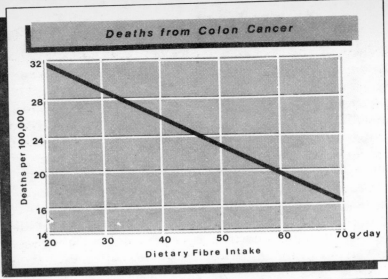

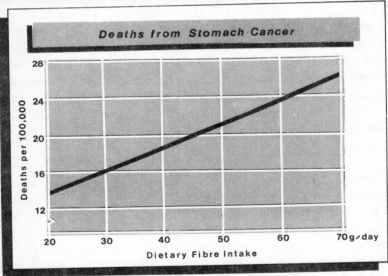

Figs. 10 and 11* Fig. 10 shows an association between fibre intake and a lower death rate from cancer of the colon. Fig. 11 shows an association between fibre intake and a higher death rate from cancer of the stomach. *Neither* constitutes evidence that dietary fibre affects health and survival.

*Source: Macdonald, I. Fibre: too much speculation, not enough facts. In D. Anderson (ed.), *A Diet of Reason*, 1986, London: The Social Affairs Unit.

difference. The only reliable direct benefit of increasing dietary fibre is the relief of constipation. Fibre relieves constipation by speeding up the time it takes for food to pass through the gut, as well as increasing its bulk. There is no evidence that speeding up transit time is beneficial to people not suffering constipation. A faster transit allows less time for digestion and absorption and therefore less time for vital minerals and trace elements to be taken up.

A high fibre diet is believed by some to protect against atherosclerosis by reducing the level of serum cholesterol. This idea has been investigated mainly in patients with abnormally high cholesterol levels. The results of these studies are again conflicting. Some show a lowering of serum cholesterol but others have failed to confirm this. Supplementing the diet with fibre seems to have most effect on serum cholesterol when the rest of the diet is high in fat. Many believe that any effect fibre may have on serum cholesterol is an indirect one and is due to a less efficient absorption of fat and a consequent reduction of overall calorie intake and, hence, body weight.

This is how an editorial in the *Lancet*, 1987, entitled *The Bran Wagon*, summarises the state of knowledge about fibre in the diet:

There is little direct evidence that increasing the intake of fibre by itself has any beneficial effect on health. The notion that people should tolerate the unpalatability of bran and its unpleasant side-effects because it will prevent diseases such as obesity, atherosclerosis, and diabetes mellitus, is founded on shaky evidence. The beneficial effects of high-fibre diets in these conditions probably result from displacement of nutrients such as fat and reduction in energy intake; the same goals can be achieved by dietary restriction without taking extra fibre. (*Lancet*, April 4th, 1987.)

Margarine

The tale of margarine is a strange one. In the United Kingdom, until the mid-1970s, margarine had made a poor showing alongside butter, partly because it did not taste as nice and partly because it bore the stigma of relative poverty. By 1980, however, soft margarine had become as popular as butter and its popularity continued to grow, and that of butter to decline, so that in the 1980s margarine became the clear winner. Clever marketing capitalised on the health boom, and the supposed health-giving qualities of polyunsaturated fats in margarine were plugged to great effect.

Before assessing the dietary value of margarine it is necessary to make a brief excursion into the chemistry of fats.

Saturated and unsaturated fatty acids

The fats we eat are made up of different combinations and mixtures of *fatty acids*. Fatty acids are chemical compounds containing the elements hydrogen, oxygen and carbon, the carbon atoms appearing in chains that vary in length. It is differences in the characteristics of the carbon chains that determine whether a fatty acid is saturated or unsaturated. Fig. 12 is a schematic illustration of the carbon chains in four different fatty acids.

Fig. 12 shows that carbon atoms 'need' four links, or bonds, with other atoms. Stearic acid (A in the Fig.) is said to be saturated since the carbon chain has as many bonds with hydrogen as is possible. There are no points along the chain where more hydrogen atoms could attach—it is thus 'saturated' with hydrogen atoms. Oleic acid (B) is not saturated with hydrogen because there is one point in the chain where a double bond exists between two carbon atoms at the expense of hydrogen. Because there is only *one* point, this is a *mono*unsaturated fatty acid. Linoleic acid (C), however, has two double bonds in the carbon chain, and docosahexaenoic acid (D) has six. More than one double

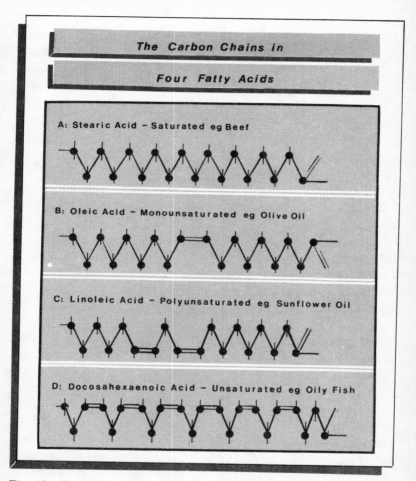

The Carbon Chains in

Four Fatty Acids

A: Stearic Acid – Saturated eg Beef

B: Oleic Acid – Monounsaturated eg Olive Oil

C: Linoleic Acid – Polyunsaturated eg Sunflower Oil

D: Docosahexaenoic Acid – Unsaturated eg Oily Fish

Fig. 12   Four fatty acids. A is the saturated *stearic acid*, found in beef and other animal fats; B is the monounsaturated *oleic acid*, found for example in olive oil; C is the polyunsaturated *linoleic acid*, found in corn oil and other vegetable oils; and D is the highly unsaturated *docosahexaenoic acid*, found in fish oils.

bond denotes a *poly*unsaturated fatty acid, and docosa-hexaenoic acid, a fish oil, is less saturated than linoleic acid: it is highly unsaturated.

No naturally occurring fat is composed of a single pure fatty acid—all fats contain mixtures of saturated, mono-unsaturated and polyunsaturated fatty acids. Animal fats have a high percentage of saturated fatty acids and vegetable fats a high percentage of unsaturated fatty acids.

Vegetable fats, because they are high in unsaturated fatty acids, have a lower melting point than animal fats and are usually called oils. Another important difference is that fats containing a high proportion of saturated fatty acids are more stable than those high in unsaturated fatty acids. The latter react with air and this is what causes them to become rancid fairly fast.

Margarines are manufactured from vegetable and fish oils, both of which are naturally high in polyunsaturated fatty acids. The raw material—the oil itself—is unsuitable as a substitute for butter for two reasons: it is too liquid to be spreadable and it quickly goes rancid. So it has to be processed. The process used—one of the most important in the food industry—is called partial hydrogenation. It involves introducing hydrogen atoms at the points of unsaturation (the double bonds) in the carbon chain. So the hitherto unsaturated fatty acids are artificially made progressively saturated, and as a result the end product—the margarine—often bears little resemblance to the natural oils used as the raw material.

Something else happens to fatty acids during the process of partial hydrogenation. As well as causing unsaturated fatty acids to become saturated, other new substances not present in the original mix of oils are produced. These are known as *trans*unsaturated fatty acids and are formed from unsaturated fatty acids. While they are chemically the same as their unsaturated originals, they differ from them in that the geometric shape of the molecule has been changed by the process. In effect, it has been twisted. Transunsaturated fatty acids are never found in natural vegetable and fish oils, and only in tiny quantities in some animal fats. The amount of transunsaturated fatty acids in margarines varies according to the brand, from about five per cent up to about 50 per cent in some cheaper brands. This is very much more than that found anywhere in nature and anywhere else in the diet. Concern about this has been expressed by several nutritionists: some argue that until more is known about the effect of transunsaturated fatty acids in the body they should properly be regarded as a food additive.[15]

Whatever may be said about the advantages of margarine, one thing is clear: 'pure' the parent oils may be, but the aggressive chemistry to which they are subjected often results in a product that is far from pure and whose effects on health are not yet understood.

Transunsaturated fatty acids are widely believed to behave like saturated fatty acids in the body. This fact alone should make one wary of manufacturers' claims about the polyunsaturated content of their products. Counting transunsaturated fatty acids as saturated fatty acids makes some brands look more like animal fats than the vegetable and fish oils that were their origins.

Fatty acids are digested, transported in the blood, and stored as 'depot fat'—the body's main reserve of energy. In times of exertion and stress it is important that these reserves are made quickly available to meet a sudden demand. During a heart attack the pulse may rise to three or four times the normal rate and energy requirement becomes critical. Some authors are concerned that transunsaturated fatty acids in stored body fat represent a less accessible energy resource than the other more natural fatty acids.

Post-mortem data published by Leo Thomas and his colleagues in Wales are consistent with this viewpoint. When post-mortem examinations are made of people who died from heart disease, a greater amount of transunsaturated fatty acid is found to be present in their body depot fat than in that of people who died from other causes. The authors explain this on the basis that 'the cases (those dead from heart disease) had consumed—by fortuitous selection of margarine brand—a higher amount of hydrogenated marine oil particularly of a certain type than had the controls (those dead from other causes).'[16]

It is also worth noting that in one of these studies, patients who had died from heart disease had *lower* concentrations of fatty acids 'characteristic of ruminant animal fat (i.e. saturated fats)' in their body fat than patients who had died from other causes.[17]

Research on the transunsaturated fatty acid content of margarines is not yet sufficiently advanced to allow any definite conclusions. But there is certainly some reason to call into question the value of the more heavily processed margarines as a 'health food'.[15]

Polyunsaturated fats

Vegetable oils and fish oils provide us with polyunsaturated fats in the diet. Some of these are called *essential fatty acids* because they are like vitamins: they are essential for healthy functioning but they are not made in sufficient quantity by the body. The main essential fatty acid is linoleic acid (see Fig. 12, p. 65).

The belief that our diet is made healthier by substituting polyunsaturated fats for saturated fats has become extremely popular and has been taken up and used to great effect in the food industry. 'High in polyunsaturates' is almost a slogan in the advertising of margarines and dairy products. Polyunsaturated fats supposedly have a favourable effect on the balance between LDL and HDL cholesterol, lowering the level in the blood of the 'bad' LDL and raising that of the 'good' HDL-cholesterol. The evidence for a favourable effect of polyunsaturates at first glance appears more firmly footed than that concerned with those aspects of diet we have considered so far. It goes as follows:

1 Eskimos and certain other fish-eating communities have a low rate of heart disease. (It will not be necessary to restate the argument that these correlations on their own are not sufficient evidence of causes.)

2 An Edinburgh-based group has conducted a series of experiments analysing the linoleic acid in body tissues. They consistently found a lower concentration of linoleic acid in people with early heart disease compared with healthy people.[18]

3 Some powerful biochemical effects of fish oils have been shown at the level of the cell. It is thought likely that fish oils inhibit blood clotting and hence reduce the risk of thrombosis. Fish oils are also believed to have an anti-inflammatory effect on conditions such as arthritis by suppressing the action of certain cells in the immune system.[19]

4 Most importantly, five large intervention studies have shown that modifying the diet so as to increase polyunsaturated fats from vegetable oils and decrease saturated fats from meat and dairy products can indeed cause a reduction in serum LDL-cholesterol levels in people who have suffered a heart attack.[20]

But (and there always seems to be a 'but' when drawing conclusions from studies of diet), no reduction in mortality from heart disease and no reduction in overall mortality was achieved by any of the modifications to the diet in any of the five studies mentioned in the last point. Furthermore, their findings raise some alarm with regard to side-effects of the modified diets. The consumption of large amounts of polyunsaturated fats (mainly linoleic acid) was considered undesirable by the investigators in three of these studies and was actually abandoned in one of them. In the study carried out in Sydney, Australia, in which the health of 458 men aged 30–39 was tracked for up to seven years, the number of deaths was slightly higher in the group consuming the polyunsaturated fat diet.[20]

The advantages of radically modifying the diet, even when this is known to have biochemical consequences such as lowering LDL-cholesterol, once again show themselves open to considerable doubt. Concern has been voiced that a big increase in the consumption of vegetable and fish oils might lead to the premature ageing of skin cells, to vulnerability to infections and to some forms of cancer because of the effects these polyunsaturates have on the immune system.[21]

Research on the benefits of supplementing the diet with fish oils is still at an early stage. Fish oils are rich in highly unsaturated fatty acids (such as docosahexaenoic acid— Fig. 12, p. 65) and the hope has been expressed that they have lowering effects not just on serum cholesterol and blood clotting but also on blood pressure. A prospective intervention study is needed to establish their potential for health, but such studies are expensive and take a long time, and we have seen how equivocal and disillusioning are the results of those that have so far been done. It may be that the hopes for fish oil as a prophylactic will be vindicated, but similar equally fervent hopes for other components of the diet have not been supported in the past. Perhaps looking to restrict or enrich a particular dietary factor on the grounds of a specific biochemical property misses the point that digestion—the absorption and transport of foods, the profile of metabolic products and the dispersal and clearance of these products in the body—is a more complex business than this presupposes. Our knowledge of how all this happens is still relatively crude. We do need essential fatty acids, but probably not in vast quantities.

Conclusion

Scientists are trained to study phenomena in isolation, under controlled, clinical conditions. The desire to isolate a single aspect of the diet, and to show that it is good or bad, has shown itself to be an overwhelmingly attractive one and has resulted in the most elaborate and expensive experiments in the history of medicine.

Despite inaccurate and sometimes irresponsible reporting, looked at closely, research to find the ideal diet seems like the search for the Holy Grail. Studies with healthy people have disappointed researchers hoping for clear, universal costs and benefits to health from specific dietary changes. None have so far shown up any single component of food, given a varied diet, as good or bad for the healthy individual. If a person suffers from very high blood pressure, then reducing salt intake may carry some benefit. If someone has excessive levels of LDL-cholesterol, they may be correctly advised to bias their diet away from saturated and towards polyunsaturated fats. However, the experiments that have been done on changing the diets of high risk individuals cast some doubt on whether even these recommendations are always right.

For the healthy person there is no proof at all that eating saturated fat, cholesterol and salt is necessarily bad, and there is no proof that eating margarine, polyunsaturated fat and fibre is necessarily good. The enormous research literature on each of these aspects of food is a minefield of inconsistency and contradiction, as it is with other aspects of the diet not discussed here, such as coffee and sugar.[22] All the experiments with healthy people and many of those with unhealthy people designed to *test* these hypotheses have turned up negative results—i.e. they have actually shown that no overall benefit is to be had from such dietary changes. Radical changes in the diet *can* influence details of body chemistry, but it has yet to be shown that any of these influences are enduring and beneficial to the non-patient. The healthy body's own complicated internal chemistry seems to react to, compensate for and often override even quite gross changes in the diet.

Experience clearly tells us that excess can be bad.

Alcoholism, obsessive under-eating (anorexia) and obsessive over-eating (bulemia) carry their own well-known dangers, as does being heavily overweight. Evidence is building up that lack of exercise is a bad thing. But there is nothing in the literature to suggest that within these limits it is not correct to let your appetite be your guide. Indeed, why else would appetite and taste exist if they were not to inform of the specific needs of a specific individual at a specific moment?

The most significant and unexpected showing of studies on diet has been the implication of side-effects—signs that the benefits of a dietary recommendation based on a considered chain of biochemical causes and effects appear to be offset by unexpected disadvantages. How reminiscent of treatment with drugs this is! Scarcely any drug is without side-effects, blood pressure- and cholesterol-lowering drugs being no exception. *None* of the major intervention studies concerned with blood cholesterol, either those done to test a cholesterol-lowering drug, or those done to test a cholesterol-lowering diet, have shown any overall benefit in terms of mortality. Several of those in which a diet high in polyunsaturates was prescribed have produced undesirable side-effects—even a higher death rate in the group treated. What is the point of going against a person's own preferences and tampering with the diet if this has no overall effect on health and may even prove disadvantageous in unexpected ways?

Chapter 3

PERSONALITY AND ILLNESS

The 'external' theory of health

The studies of diet and health reviewed in the previous two chapters are all founded on a common belief: that there are specific identifiable components of the normal diet that have good or bad effects on health, and that these effects are universal. We might call this the *external* theory of health: the external composition of the foods we swallow has a one-to-one relation with our physical well-being. It is easy to see why such a theory is so attractive to researchers and doctors. If it is true, it opens the way for a set of formulae regarding what we should and should not eat, which are easily followed and will automatically result in the improved health and longevity of populations.

But as we have seen, simple formulae about diet and health fail to hold up. One by one they are embarrassed by the facts and one by one they fail to support the parent axiom—that health can be universally and profoundly affected by fiddling with individual constituents of the normal diet. A great excess of anything will act like a poison in the body, but apart from this rather obvious fact research so far does not support the external theory.

The 'internal' theory of health

In opposition to the external theory is the idea that what the body does with nutrients entering the stomach is of much greater overall importance than the composition of the diet itself. Cholesterol provides a good example of this principle. When a cholesterol-rich meal is eaten the mechanisms that transport, metabolise and dispose of cholesterol, as well as the body's own cholesterol factories, are adjustable and will tend to maintain cholesterol in the blood at a roughly constant, healthy level. They act in concert as a complex homeostatic device and there are good reasons to believe that the efficacy of this homeostasis is itself influenced by other bodily systems such as hormones. The picture that is beginning to build up, of numerous communicating, interacting and mutually regulating mechanisms, is indeed a complex one. Our knowledge of it is far from complete but is sufficient to be able to say these systems exist and are very powerful.

The external theory of the body as a passive responder —a universal standard reactor—to concentrations of cholesterol, fat, salt, fibre, or whatever, in the diet, at best underestimates and at worst completely ignores this complicated and delicate internal chemistry. The idea that such chemistry has prepotence, and that within the range of what are considered normal (i.e. non toxic) diets internal forces override external (dietary) ones, will be referred to as the *internal theory* of health.

There are signs that the internal theory has a growing following not only among people seeking treatment, but also among practitioners and researchers. Too many drugs have unpleasant side-effects and an increasing number of people when they are unwell now prefer to seek treatment from alternative sources. Holistic medicine in its various forms is attracting both public and professional interest. The words 'autoaggressive' and 'systemic' are increasingly to be found in journal articles concerned with pathological states. Both these terms imply that a disease is the result of disruption in the normal health-protecting mechanisms of the healthy body, in particular, the immune system. Heart disease and cancer have both been discussed as having autoaggressive origins.[1,2]

The idea that the chemistry of the healthy body is thrown

out of balance when a person is run down or stressed goes back to Hippocrates and has always been informally acknowledged by physicians. But what are the conditions of our normal healthy internal chemistry? Precisely in what circumstances does this break down and leave us vulnerable to disease?

There is more than one way of approaching this question. We can look at diseased tissue at a microscopic level and try to trace it back, step by step, to its origins. Doing this will with luck provide us with answers in the precise language of biochemistry. For example, a high level in the blood of the hormone noradrenaline is thought to disrupt normal fat metabolism and promote the deposit of fat in coronary arteries. Noradrenaline and atherosclerosis are physical things and the precision of the biochemical analysis comes from our being able to measure them and express the relation between them reasonably accurately.

The other way to study the conditions of health is to look for circumstances in which the body's normal healthy functions break down and the person becomes ill. This method is different in that we are not restricted to the language of biochemistry. In fact we are not really restricted at all: we can use the language of psychiatry, psychology, sociology, religion or even magic to capture and describe this circumstance.

This chapter and the following one concentrate on the psychology of illness. In doing so a certain degree of the precision of the biochemical approach is inevitably sacrificed. What is gained is the freedom to look at health and illness, logically, in relation to the way people live, and this allows insights that we could never have if we were confined to pure biochemistry. 'Stress' is an intuitive, metaphorical kind of word. The study of the psychology of stress and the relation of stress to illness is basically an effort to define stress more tightly and establish the conditions of its influence on health. High levels of noradrenaline and other chemicals in the blood are brought on by stress. We need psychology to arrive at an understanding of the nature of stress.

THE PSYCHOLOGY OF STRESS

Does stress really pose a serious threat to health? If so, in what circumstances? Is it something we can avoid or help others to avoid? Before we can answer these questions we must look at the evidence connecting aspects of people's lives and lifestyles with a critical breakdown in their health. It is in this evidence that the clues to the essence and the avoidance of stress lie.

Are there illness-prone personalities?

The first major group of studies appeared in the 1940s and 1950s under the cloak of psychoanalysis. A cluster of unrelated conditions—asthma, hypertension, ulcers, irritable bowel, migraine, low back pain and some skin disorders—were regarded as 'psychosomatic'; they were thought to be physical manifestations of an underlying psychological tension.

Freud provided the starting point for much of this work. At the centre of his theory is the notion of *repression*: certain needs and fears, often originating in childhood experiences, are banished from the adult consciousness into the realm of the unconscious. Physical symptoms were believed to be the symbolic expression of these repressed emotions. Asthma, for example, was seen as the expression of deep-rooted inhibitions about communicating with other people. Hypertension was represented as the result of repressed hostility, and ulcers were seen as the consequence of frustrated desires to seek help.

The evidence for these connections was drawn from case histories of patients. Here is an extract from a typical such case history of a 35-year-old American man with a duodenal ulcer, reported in 1943:

The picture of this man was that of an energetic, hard-working, 'successful' person with marked repressions and retarded emotional development, indicated by his strong attachment to his mother, afraid to face marriage and compromising the situation by maintaining an engagement for an indefinite period, meanwhile giving a great many reasons, which were obviously not good reasons, for avoiding marriage. Apparently the affair produced a conflict between his attachment to his mother and his desire to establish an independent home and to attain a proper masculine (heterosexual) goal.

His deference to his mother's wishes and his attitude of excessive morality and goodness indicated unconscious strivings of passivity and dependency, while his energetic pursuit of business and indefinite 'engagement' to a girl to whom his mother objected indicated his conscious efforts at accomplishment and independence. Such a conflict refuted his denial of any worry or stress apart from indigestion and showed how necessary an understanding of unconscious strivings was to appreciate the forceful psychic influences that were at work in this patient.

Summary

A young man with duodenal ulcer developed a large gastric hemorrhage. No obvious emotional factors were apparent but personality study showed conflict between unconscious strivings of dependency and the conscious struggle for independence and success. This was brought to the surface by indecision over a marriage situation.

(From *Psychosomatic Medicine* ed. E. Weiss and O. S. English, W. B. Saunders: Philadelphia, 1943.)

A demand for scientific rigour in the 1960s saw this type of study fall out of fashion. The analysis of case histories was criticised as too vague and subjective a standard on which to base theories about the psychological origins of illness. Because these analyses rested on the description of matters that were unconscious, and therefore *in principle* unavailable for public scrutiny and verification by the scientific community, they were widely dismissed as unscientific. Nevertheless, although many reports are long and rambling, they make interesting reading and there is some consistency among them. The treatments meted out by these psychoanalyst doctors were tailored to an individual's personal needs, as these were construed, and frequently, if the reports are to be believed, they resulted in complete or partial remission of the patient's symptoms. In this sense they represent small scale but genuine and successful intervention studies. Opponents of the psychoanalytic approach explain these successes as a placebo effect—purely the result of the doctor offering support and encouragement to the patient.

Psychoanalytic explanations will probably never be acceptable to hard scientists. However, this does not mean they are without value. They often contain useful insights and are a rich source of hypotheses as to the relation between stress and illness.

The rush in the 1960s and 1970s to study stress and illness scientifically resulted in the publication of thousands of research reports: studies of animals in the laboratory, studies of humans in the laboratory and studies of humans in natural situations. There is a curious irony about the obsession of psychologists at this time with being properly scientific. The attraction of working in the laboratory is that it offers great control and allows close measurements of physiological reactions to stress such as heart rate, blood pressure, skin resistance and noradrenaline. Mice were chosen as the unfortunate main animal model and the adopted stress technique, still used, was to rotate them on a turntable. The degree of stress was assumed to be proportional to the speed of rotation.

A bizarre assembly of techniques was devised throughout these decades to induce stress in human subjects: electric shock, having an arm immersed in freezing water, white noise, trying to solve insoluble puzzles, watching films of people being circumcised without anaesthesia, boredom, group pressure and disapproval from peers—to take just a few examples. The choice of stressor in these experiments was entirely arbitrary. So while they may be able to tell us a little about animal and human physiology they tell us nothing at all about the psychology of stress. In most cases the stresses dreamed up were artificial and far removed from the kinds of things that people suffer as the darker side of life. The context in which stress is contrived in humans in the laboratory is itself highly artificial. Volunteers or conscripts for these experiments well know they are taking part in an experiment, and whatever happens to them in the laboratory is not to be taken too seriously.

For these reasons only studies of human beings in natural situations will be considered in these chapters. These are the only studies that can cast light on the *psychology* of the stressful circumstances that constitute a threat to a person's health.

The reaction against subjectivity in psychoanalysts' case histories naturally led to a hunt for a more objective way of studying personality. The successful measurement of personality became an important prize up for the taking. But no universally accepted standard ever came out of this and there remain differences of opinion about how best to measure personality and about what aspects of personality should be studied. Despite the differences, research on personality clearly shows an association of certain traits with illness.

1 Depression

A considerable number of studies have found an association between physical illness and mental depression.[3] The finding is reinforced by other studies which have shown depressed states to be associated with disturbances in the normal healthy balance of certain hormones and in the healthy performance of the immune system.[4]

However, an association between depression and physical illness, without further theoretical explication, does not tell us a great deal because depression and illness, while not exactly synonymous, are very closely related concepts. Being depressed is so much part of being ill that it will always be hard to say whether depression led to illness or whether illness brought on the depressed state. The value in trying to disentangle this chicken-and-egg puzzle may in the end turn out to be somewhat limited. Even if we can predict who will become ill in a healthy sample of people on the basis of scores on a scale of depression, there is the possibility that the disease is there in a latent, as yet undiagnosed, 'pre-clinical', state.

Nonetheless, there is one study, of a large sample of middle-aged American men, which might be considered exempt from this criticism because of the long period of time over which the men were studied.[5] In 1957–8, depression as a personality trait was measured in 2,018 employees of the Western Electric Company, using one of the best-established American questionnaire scales (the MMPI). Twenty years later, high scorers on the original depression scale were seen to have suffered twice the incidence of fatal cancers compared with the others. This association was independent of age, smoking, alcohol intake, occupational status, family history of cancer, body weight and level of serum cholesterol. The authors interpret these findings as consistent with the hypothesis that mental depression 'might promote the development and spread of malignant neoplasms'.

2   Cancer and the bottling up of emotions

A much more challenging theme, to emerge with some consistency, is a tendency among people at risk of developing certain forms of cancer to show an abnormal pattern in the expression of their emotions. The observation that cancer patients suppress, repress and deny negative feelings such as anger, depression and guilt, has been made by numerous clinicians specialising in cancer, and was first proposed as a formal hypothesis by Kissen in the 1960s in relation to lung cancer patients.[6] Kissen compared 161 patients who were diagnosed as suffering from lung cancer with 174 patients diagnosed as having less serious illnesses, and concluded that cancer patients showed a 'diminished outlet for emotional discharge', during both childhood and adulthood.

Other studies of patients with cancer supported this hypothesis.[7] Some authors even ventured the suggestion that the repressed and denied emotions in the cancer patient found physical expression in the cancer itself.

Repressed and denied emotions have a tendency to come out in camouflaged ways, in dreams and in the things a person thinks and says. One particularly interesting study[8] showed this in a group of women attending a clinic under suspicion of breast cancer. Before they were diagnosed, the 62 women were interviewed by a physician, and what people said in the interview was analysed for the use of certain types of word—words denoting hopelessness and words related to cancer and death. Both 'cancer' and 'death' were used more often by the 27 women who were ultimately found to have cancer than the others who were found to be free of the disease. But the most interesting thing about this finding is that these words were used in a metaphorical sense—for example, 'I was tickled to death', and 'he'll be the death of me'. Is what we are seeing in this study an image of a tendency to repress and deny associated with cancer: knowledge of the cancer being kept strictly unconscious but being betrayed by this so-called 'lexical leakage'?

Studies of emotions in people who know they have cancer raise special problems. Communication to the patient of a diagnosis of cancer is itself a highly emotive matter. It is bound to unleash powerful emotions—emotions which are not common among people leading normal healthy lives, or even among patients with less serious diseases. The problem of separating the emotional impact of such a grave diagnosis from the measure of emotion itself means it is difficult to know quite what to make of some of these clinical observations and findings. Certainly, in those studies where the measure of emotional tendency was made shortly after the diagnosis of cancer, it can reasonably be argued, as indeed it was, that suppression, repression and denial are natural first reactions to such distressing news.

Steven Greer and his team, working at the Faith Courtauld Unit at King's College Hospital, London, carried out some trials in the 1970s, which took into account this source of bias.[9] They too studied women with suspicious lumps on their breasts, before it was known whether these were cancerous or benign. They found it was possible to predict cancer cases on the basis of how a person expressed anger, especially in younger patients. Those who turned out to have cancer exhibited an abnormal tendency: most of the time they would suppress their feelings and deny that they were in any way anxious, but once in a while they would give vent to intemperate outbursts. The authors make an interesting comment: 'in life, as well as in the test situation (presenting for surgery), they may well be reluctant to appear in any way socially unacceptable.'

Exactly the same finding was reported in a similar study of women admitted to a clinic in Heidelberg for breast biopsies.[10] One of the distinguishing characteristics of those who turned out to have cancer was 'emotional suppression with sudden outbursts'. The women in the London study diagnosed as having cancer underwent mastectomies and were traced by the research team for a further ten years. Some women accepted the disease stoically and of these 75 per cent had died within this time. Others adopted a 'hostile and fighting' attitude and of these only 30 per cent had died in the ten years. An American study confirmed this latter finding: survival in breast cancer patients went hand in hand with the expression of unpleasant emotions like anxiety, feelings of alienation and hostility.[11] The opposite repressive personality profile has also been linked to the speed at which breast cancer spreads.[12]

Essentially the same relation between personality and disease was found in women with early signs of cervical cancer.[13] The susceptible group were described as 'passive, pessimistic, conforming, avoiding and somatically anxious', while those who turned out more resilient to the disease were 'more optimistic and employed more active coping styles'.

This relation is not unique to women. The same thing was reported for men undergoing surgery for colorectal cancer.[14] 'denial was significantly associated with poor outcome whereas fighting spirit was associated with a good outcome.'

These associations do not necessarily reflect underlying causes. The women who were more open about their emotions may, for instance, have taken greater care in looking after themselves. However, a further clue is provided by studies that have shown a relationship between mood and the workings of the immune system. The immune system contains all the body's mechanisms for fighting infection and is immensely complex. It is also known to play an important part in the control of cancer by spotting cancer cells in the bloodstream and destroying them before they have a chance to lodge in tissue and amass into tumours. This finding has led Harvard psychologist, David McClelland, to propose that when strong feelings are bottled up and not dissipated by being let out, the individual is the victim of chronically high levels of stress hormones, like adrenaline, noradrenaline and cortisol. Such hormones are known to have an unfavourable effect on the immune system by inhibiting some of its health-protecting mechanisms—they are immuno-suppressive.[15,16]

More direct evidence that repression is linked with changes in immune function comes from the State University of California. This team, comprising a psychologist, a psychiatrist and a physician, succeeded in showing that there was a depletion of certain cells which make up an essential part of the immune system in repressors.[17]

Eighteen well-designed studies on the link between emotional expression and cancer have so far been done. A recent review of these ends thus: 'This review of 18 studies supports the consensus that emotional expression may be directly implicated in cancer onset and progression.'[18]

There is an intuitive ring to the idea that giving vent to one's feelings and letting it all out is healthy. When someone has suffered a tragic loss he or she is encouraged to weep, and there is a suggestion that emotional weeping has the physically beneficial effect of ridding the body of toxins.[19] The same principle provides the cornerstone of certain forms of group thereapy, where situations are deliberately set up to provoke dramatic encounters between individuals.

A repressive outside environment also appears conducive to the development of cancer. A study over a ten-year period of the inhabitants of a small town in Yugoslavia, found that being a 'passive receiver of repression', where here 'repression' means the restrictive interference of others, predicted the incidence of cancers of all types.[20]

The definitive test of the theory would of course be to take a sample of patients with early cancer and provide half of them with training in the expression of emotion while using the other half as a control group. If the suppression of feelings contributes to the development and aggravation of malignancy, then the group given training (assuming this is effective) might be expected to do better and live longer than the others. However, setting up such a trial would be difficult in view of the sensitive nature of the cancer diagnosis and the possibility that the control group was missing out on a potentially beneficial form of treatment. A big preventive trial using healthy volunteers would be unwieldy because of the huge resources it would require. So it may prove ultimately impossible to set up an intervention study. But there is sufficient agreement among studies and clinical reports to conclude that the relation between cancer and the suppression of emotion is a real one, and one that deserves further investigation.

Blood pressure, too, it seems, is subject to the same potentially harmful effect. When experienced anger is not expressed, blood pressure is raised.[21] The physiology behind this relation is more easily understood. When a person becomes angry, heart rate increases and there is constriction of the blood vessels in the skin and in the viscera, and this will tend to raise blood pressure. If there is movement, this is accompanied by a dilation of blood vessels in the muscles responsible, which can counter the increase in blood pressure caused by vasoconstriction in other areas and increased cardiac output. This may provide an explanation of the classic finding that London bus drivers have a higher rate of heart disease than bus conductors.[22] Driving a bus is a frustrating business and the poor driver is confined to his seat at moments when he would probably like to stamp around and punch the air.

3 The coronary-prone or Type-A person

The coronary-prone or, as it was first called, the Type-A personality, again has its origins in the observations of physicians. The cardiologist Sir William Osler in 1910 typified the angina case as 'vigorous in mind and body, the ambitious man, the indicator of whose engine is always at full speed ahead.'

In the 1950s, two cardiologists in San Francisco, Ray Rosenman and Meyer Friedman, embarked on a systematic programme of research on this aggressive, striving disposition. They called it (for no particular reason) the Type-A pattern. Type-A people show the following cluster of traits: they have an overriding need to achieve, they work constantly against the clock and often in the face of real or imagined opposition from other people; they are highly competitive, they deny (note, *denial* again) getting tired and they become hostile if they perceive or imagine impediments to their progress.[23]

Often when I have lectured on the Type-A pattern it has been possible to discern a gasp of self-recognition from the audience: most people will recognise some of these traits as characteristics of themselves some of the time. But the point about the Type-A person is that he *never* seems able to relax and turn off from an obsessive preoccupation with self-advancement. The Type-B is his opposite and is relaxed and unmotivated to the point of lethargy. The Type-A/Type B distinction is a scale rather than a strict division and most of us fall somewhere between the two extremes (Fig. 13).

Friedman and Rosenman developed a clever way of measuring the amount of Type-A in a person, using a structured interview. Like any other, the interview consists

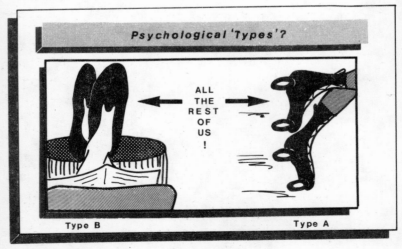

Fig. 13   Type-A and Type-B are extremes.

of asking a subject a list of questions, in this case things such as, 'How do you react when you have to wait in a queue?' or 'How do you feel when you are driving behind someone going too slow?' The actual answers people give to these questions are considered less significant than the way they react to the interview situation itself. The whole procedure is designed to be maximally irritating so as to elicit the tell-tale Type-A behaviours. People have to come for their interviews at an awkward time. They are kept waiting and when they are eventually seen they are asked questions by an interviewer who is unfriendly, incompetent, interrupting and uninterested. The interview is scored 75 per cent on the style of a person's reaction to it and only 25 per cent on the answers given.

The typical response of an extreme Type-A person in this situation is anything but relaxed. He becomes agitated, irritated and speaks with a fast, loud, clipped voice; he tries to control and speed up the interview by butting in when the interviewer pauses; he recounts difficult and frustrating incidents with an emotional intensity as if he was reliving the event. The Type-B person speaks slowly and does not get ruffled. It is only a small minority at the Type-A end of the scale who seem especially prone to heart disease.

Type-A is not a pure characteristic, like anger or grief. It is a mix of things which, although they intuitively hang together, are in fact independent. Hostility, for example, can obviously exist independently of the rest of the Type-A characteristics, as can a high motivation to achieve at one's work. What defines the Type-A person is the combination of these factors and their pre-eminence in his life.

The evidence linking Type-A behaviour with risk of heart disease is impressive, though not unanimous. Since 1960 this has been a very fashionable area of research and there have been numerous hypotheses about Type-A and many hundreds of studies. The fact that these do not show universal agreement is to be expected when the measurement of Type-A itself, like all measures of personality, has a certain inbuilt flabbiness. It is not like measuring, say, level of LDL-cholesterol using calibrated instruments. No two interviews are ever quite the same: the same social situation can never be reproduced exactly. Although voice analysers and video recorders are often used to monitor a subject's reactions in an interview, and although great care is taken to ensure that ratings of speech patterns, hostility and so forth are as objective as possible, the measurement of Type-A can never be anything like as objective as a biochemical measurement.

Research is further complicated by the fact that there are alternative methods of assessing Type-A using straight questionnaires which subjects complete themselves. The most popular of these is the Jenkins Activity Survey.[24] This theoretically measures three factors: H—hard driving competitiveness, S—speed and impatience, and J—job involvement.

Given the variety of ways of approaching and scoring the Type-A characteristic and the imperfections in each one of these, it is surprising to see so much consensus. A solid core of studies has shown extreme Type-A behaviour to be a risk factor for heart disease in men,[25] although exactly what this means is still the subject of intense debate. The main evidence comes from three prospective studies in which measurements of Type-A behaviour were made in large samples of basically healthy individuals (mainly men), who were followed for a number of years over which time statistics relating to health and mortality were collected.

The Western Collaborative Group Study[26] was begun in 1960 and the health of 3,154 initially healthy men was studied over a 22-year period. After an average of 8.5 years it was found that, compared to Type-Bs, twice the number of men originally classed as Type-A on the basis of a structured interview had developed some form of heart disease. When Type-A profiles were analysed according to their component parts, 'hostility' emerged as the factor most powerfully related to heart disease.[27] Post-mortem examination of those men who had died from causes other than heart disease revealed a greater degree of atherosclerosis in the major heart vessels of Type-A men. After 22 years the relation between Type-A and heart disease was no longer apparent,[28] although Type-A men over the age of 60 did report more symptoms of general ill-health than their Type-B counterparts.[29] Twenty-two years is a long time in anyone's life, and it is to be expected that people and the situations in which they find themselves will change significantly over such a time.

The Framingham Study,[30] in which 750 men and 580 women were followed up over a ten-year period, also showed that being Type-A doubled the risk of heart disease. In both these studies Type-A predicted heart disease independently of the traditional risk factors—blood pressure, serum cholesterol, smoking and age—each one of which was on its own a highly significant predictor. Type-A was also seen to amplify the pathogenic effect of these other risk factors.[31]

The French-Belgium Collaborative Study,[32] the third in this series, came up with broadly similar findings. In a sample of 3,000 male factory workers and civil servants, Type-A behaviour predicted fatal and non-fatal heart attacks, sudden cardiac deaths and the overall incidence of heart disease.

A hostile disposition is a main component of the Type-A profile. Two further prospective studies showed hostility on its own to be a risk factor for heart disease over periods of 20 and 25 years.[33,34] It is worth noting that hostility scores also predicted overall mortality in both studies. Some studies have failed to demonstrate a relation between Type-A and heart disease: in particular, those of patients with suspected cardiac problems. In one, Type-A behaviour was evaluated in 519 Australians one day prior to angiography —a scan of the main vessels around the heart. Both a structured interview and a questionnaire were used, but neither revealed a relation between Type-A and extent of disease as this was shown from the scans.[35] An exactly similar study of 2,289 Americans did find a relation, but only in young people.[36] In general, the results of this type of study have been mixed.

Studies of patients awaiting angiography have become quite popular with researchers because they are relatively easy to carry out. In interpreting their findings it must be borne in mind that subjects are all people suspected of having some level of heart disease, and it may be that this is too narrow a spectrum on the health-disease scale for any effect of Type-A to show up. The failure of some studies to demonstrate an association could be due to the inherent roughness of the psychological assessment. However, taking them as a whole, the great majority of studies of Type-A and hostility do show a link between these personalities and heart disease.

Two intervention studies recently reported in the *British Medical Journal* lend further strong support to this conclusion. Professor Michael Marmot, Dr Chandra Patel and their colleagues actually tried to *prevent* illness in a sample of 192 men who were high risk cases for heart disease.[37] All of them had two or more of the following three risk factors—high blood pressure, high serum cholesterol, and smoking more than ten cigarettes a day. Everyone was given advice in the form of health education leaflets but only half the sample had group sessions once a week for eight weeks, during which they were taught breathing exercises, relaxation and meditation techniques and management of stress. After eight weeks there was a significantly greater reduction in both systolic and diastolic blood pressure in the group given relaxation training compared with the group not given this training. When blood pressures were measured again four years later, this difference still persisted. It was not due to any difference in smoking habit because the number of cigarettes smoked in each group was the same. Moreover, after four years, fewer people in the group given the training had angina and fewer were receiving treatment for hypertension and its complications. The incidence of heart disease and fatal heart attacks was also significantly lower in the trained group.

Recently, as a small part of a very large project organised by the Medical Research Council,[38] the same team used the same technique—relaxation training once a week for eight weeks—to see if this could help patients suffering from mild hypertension. The original study included 17,345 men and women in 192 general practices throughout Britain. The principal aim was to assess the effects of treatment of mild hypertension with two drugs, and the effects of coming off the drugs after a while. For six years people took either the drugs or dummy placebos. In the second phase of the study, a subgroup of 2,765 people was allocated either to continue receiving drug or placebo, or to discontinue this. At this stage there were therefore four groups. In the third phase, a sub-subgroup of just 134 people was allocated either to receive relaxation training or not. The study of relaxation therefore set out to compare two groups of people: those receiving training and those not, but within each of these two groups four different histories of drug taking were represented.

Results showed that one year after the end of the trial those who had stopped receiving the drugs continued to show the reduced blood pressure that the drugs had caused, but only if they had received relaxation training. Moreover, blood pressure was reduced further by relaxation training in those who continued with drug or placebo.

Both these studies provide evidence of a beneficial effect on blood pressure of relaxation training. Neither was concerned directly with trying to modify Type-A behaviour but it is a reasonable assumption that training people to relax works in the direction of training them away from any Type-A habits they might have.

In America, programmes aimed directly at modifying Type-A behaviour have proved successful, both in terms of altering Type-A traits and in reducing the risk of heart disease and death, at least in middle-aged male volunteers.[39] Techniques vary from study to study. Some involve pure education, while others, like the two British trials just described, incorporate training and exercises in relaxation. The discovery that this kind of training can be an effective substitute for drugs in the long-term treatment of essential hypertension has also been confirmed.[40]

The success of these intervention studies is very important to the *internal theory* of health. Aside from the obvious implication for clinical practice, together with the other studies of Type-A behaviour they constitute sound scientific evidence for the involvement of psychological factors in the causation of hypertension and heart disease.

It has to be admitted that the exact nature of the 'psychological factors' influencing blood pressure and heart disease is by no means finally resolved. The original Type-A hypothesis has provided us with a good workable starting point, but the inconsistencies in findings mean that it will definitely not be the end of the theoretical line. Even the concept of hostility is not without its own ambiguity. Anger can be expressed against others, against situations and against oneself; it can come in outbursts or it can fester. We still have a fair way to go to understand just what is going on in the relation between personality and heart disease.

Nor is it clear that the Type-A pattern relates exclusively to risk of heart disease. A high incidence of Type-A traits has been reported in groups of patients with peptic ulcers, allergies and respiratory infections.[41] In the Western Collaborative Study Type-As were found to be at greater risk also for accidents, suicide and homicide.[42]

We also know that Type-A people exhibit various atypical physiological reactions in challenging situations. They show an exaggerated response of the sympathetic nervous system—the branch of the nervous system that is automatically activated in times of stress and prepares the body for fight or flight. They also show a higher secretion of

some stress-related hormones as well as distinc[...]
wave patterns on the electroencephalograph trace[...]

We must conclude that there is something imp[...]
behind the Type-A/heart disease relation. It is very s[...]
ficant that the intervention studies produced positive [...]
sults. Not only do these give strong support to the hypothesis, they also indicate that Type-A behaviour or whatever
lies behind it is amenable to modification; it is not intract-
able and with the right techniques can be plied into a better
style of dealing with the world and one with healthier
consequences.

Most theorists regard Type-A as a maladaptive, or
flawed, way of coping with the environment—especially
with situations that are difficult or stressful. It clearly has to
do with ambition and a need to achieve, and equally clearly
involves a certain dogged inflexibility in going about this.[44]

The popularity of this research has tended to mask some
earlier observations about the personalities of coronary-
prone individuals. Perfectionist traits have been observed
in their social lives as well as in relation to their work. They
have been described as having a strong sense of duty, as
being more than normally concerned with social correct-
ness and nicety, as being rigid and scrupulous, as over-
controlling their emotions and as possessing obsessional
traits.[45] Linking these statements with the work on Type-A,
we get the impression that this person is trying very hard to
prove something to other people, and perhaps to himself,
and is not succeeding too well. The 'Sisyphus reaction' is
yet another description that has been related to people who
suddenly die from a heart attack.[46] Sisyphus, king of
Corinth, was by legend condemned to roll an enormous
stone up a hill, only to have it roll back down again so as to
make his task impossible and unending.

Pictured as striving, over-zealous and enjoying little
sense of accomplishment and satisfaction, the Type-A or
coronary-prone person provides a good model for the
philosophical position that has become known as the

equilibrium theory of health.[47] This simply states that individuals are healthy if their capabilities are adequate to their goals; they are ill, or unhealthy, if this is not the case. They are only slightly ill if their capabilities are almost adequate and they are very ill if they are grossly inadequate.

The *equilibrium theory* is clearly insufficient as it stands. What is meant by 'goal', and how are personal goals to be measured? And what about people with very low ambition —are they never ill? How can this theory account for the cancer-prone person; the suppressor of emotions? We shall take this up in later chapters. But first we must look at another important area of research—also one that is currently getting a great deal of attention: the effects of stressful events in people's lives on their health and survival.

Chapter 4

STRESSFUL SITUATIONS AND ILLNESS

Fighting for one's life is stressful by anyone's standards, and indeed, the study of stress and its effect on humans began with men in combat, who suffered the disabling 'shell shock' of the First World War and the 'combat fatigue' of the Second. The sudden interest in stress in times of war did not spring entirely from an altruistic motive: the effectiveness of a military offensive is not helped by individuals who are incapacitated.

Yet being in active combat can have a quite different psychological effect, as these interviews with servicemen fighting in the British Falklands conflict of 1982 show:

Then I wasn't frightened any more. It was an adrenaline high. You saw all these bullets flying about you but you never thought you would be hit. It was a real high. I just thought, 'This is it, what an experience.' It was the first time I had been under fire.

It was a pleasure to fight in the Falklands with '42'. There was a fantastic spirit. The professionalism came out in those 18-year-olds. I think I was reliving a cycle of my own life, because I could remember how I came up. You became like a fox—the sight, the smell, the ear, everything's there.

(From *Sunday Times Magazine*, April, 1983)

These do not sound like the accounts of people crippled by stress; at least, if one insists on defining the situation they were in as stressful, they seem to be reacting favourably, not badly. A study made of American soldiers in active combat in Vietnam confirmed that levels of stress hormones can be lower than off-duty levels—providing there is strong comradeship.[1]

This shows just how slippery the concept of stress is. We know that different people prefer different levels of stimulation: some like a bit of danger and find it exhilarating; to others, even a trip to the shops brings on feelings of panic. Nevertheless, despite its ambiguity, the metaphor of person-under-stress is a very useful one. Research on stress and illness is mutual. Not only does a knowledge of the situations in which a person becomes vulnerable enrich our understanding of illness, it also helps refine our ideas about stress. There is no tautology in this relationship because stress is conceived psychologically and illness, physically.

In the previous chapter we identified some personality traits that are themselves sources of stress. In this chapter we look at the effects on people of stressful circumstances in their lives, especially when these are not quickly resolved and persist over a period of time.

Intuitively, the difference between stresses which are temporary and those which persist seems an important one. An occasional row with someone close, that is soon resolved, is better than continual bickering. Research confirms that enduring stresses are the ones that do the greatest harm—mainly because the individual fails to cope with the source of the stress. Failure to work through a bereavement via the natural process of mourning is a case in point.

An outstanding example of an environment that is hostile, unremitting and beyond the capacity of the individual to control or change is provided by the highly organised, highly effective, concentration camps of Nazi Germany in the 1930s and early 1940s. Perhaps the Nazis should not be singled out for their regime of terror—there are plenty of other examples of organised barbarism in the history of the world—but there are two facts that make this period of European history extraordinarily relevant to the discussion of stress and survival. One is the availability of a number of scholarly records and analyses of these times, both from survivors and from those in command. Second, there is no similar period in the history of the world (at least none of which there is an adequate record) when a programme of suffering and humiliation has been so minutely planned and successfully put into effect on such an enormous scale. The design and operation of these camps reveal a profound insight on the part of their originators into the psychology of human stress.

There exist many detailed accounts of the conditions of living in these places: the survival rate in all of them was extremely low, but there were some survivors and it is worth asking how these few were able to cope with and come through such a terrible experience when the great majority, even of those not murdered on their arrival, did not.

The first camp, at Dachau, was opened by Himmler in 1933 to house 5,000 prisoners who were an overflow from the overcrowded German prisons. The internees were predominantly criminals and people arrested for 'political' offences. They included anti-fascists, Catholics, Jews, emigrants, vagrants and homosexuals. Dachau became the model for all the camps that were subsequently to be built, and it was Theodor Eicke who, more than anyone else, shaped the character of Dachau and laid down the foundations for the others. Discipline was based on a pyramidical structure of power, with the commandant at the top and inmates who enjoyed special privileges at the bottom. The latter were mainly criminals who had been chosen to be in charge of a particular hut or a particular working party. In between were various levels of SS officers trained in the practice of subjugation through brutality at one of a number of academies set up for this purpose.

Prisoners were rounded up and housed in transit camps throughout Europe, then transported in cattle trucks to one of the specially constructed centres in Germany or Poland. They arrived to confront genocide, dreadful living conditions, infestation, disease, and brutality that was not only licensed but actively encouraged. Over and above all this, there was the ever-present threat of death by shooting or, later in the life of the camps, being sent to a gas chamber in one of the infamous 'selections'. The regime of terror began with a carefully planned series of initiations from the moment prisoners disembarked at a nearby railway station. They were beaten, stripped naked, made to take showers and had their hair shaved. The only personal effect they carried forward with them was a number tattooed on the forearm.

Living conditions were overcrowded, food insufficient and work assignments overburdening. The day was governed by innumerable gratuitous rules and punishments. The daily roll-call at dawn, a central feature of camp life, meant standing to attention sometimes for hours in the cold. The system even extended to a deliberate policy of inadequate toilet facilities. Stangl, commandant of the Polish camp at Treblinka, later openly explained the thinking behind this: the fact that prisoners were contaminated with their own excrement made it easier for the guards to regard them as subhuman and so carry out their brutal duties.[2]

On any hypothesis of stress as accumulated physical or emotional strain, one would expect the death rate from causes other than killings to be highest among those who had suffered the conditions of the camp for the longest period. But this was not the case: without exception, natural death rate, if one can call it that, was highest during the first weeks of a person's imprisonment.

Such a picture agrees with psychological evidence that long-term conditions, however stressful they might appear to an outside observer, do not inevitably result in physical breakdown. It is the person's capacity to adapt and cope that holds the key.[3] On their arrival at Auschwitz, one of the larger camps, confronted with the ferocious conditions of life and death, most prisoners went into a state of suspended belief which often lasted for weeks. 'Nightmare' and 'unreality' are the two words that, according to the analysis made by Des Pres,[4] appear most frequently in survivors' accounts of these first days and weeks—for example, 'All around us were screams, death, smoking chimneys making the air black and heavy with soot and the smell of burning bodies . . . It was just like a nightmare and it took weeks and weeks before I could really believe this was happening.'[5]

Bruno Bettelheim makes precisely the same observation: 'Not only during the transport, but for a long time to come, prisoners had to convince themselves that this was real and not just a nightmare.'[6]

But, as Victor Frankl, another survivor, points out,[7] failure sooner or later to accept the reality of life in the camp was a failure to adapt, and carried with it all the dangers that the stress-illness theory would predict. Those prisoners who recovered from the initial shock and forced themselves to admit that conditions were as bad as or worse than their most dire imaginings, developed what is referred to in survivors' accounts as a 'fighting spirit'. Note the parallel between these reports and the findings of research, in relation to cancer, on the adverse consequences of repression and denial and the favourable ones of a fighting spirit (Chapter 3).

There is also good agreement among survivors' accounts that survival was related to the adoption of some moral initiative, or goal, difficult though this was in the circumstances. This could take various forms. Sometimes a sense of commitment was found in a determination to make a record of the conditions of camp life so that later the world should come to know about them. Sometimes it was found in helping others, as is the case for this Polish woman whose job it was to index incoming prisoners at Maidenek: 'I knew that a person coming to a camp was afraid of everything and everybody, that she was distracted and terrified. The first word was so important. I decided to be patient, to answer all questions, to calm them and give them courage. My life began to hold meaning.'[8] Sometimes it was found simply in trying to keep washed and clean —not an easy task.

Failure to be realistic about camp life and in effect to become part of it by taking on a role of some kind was notoriously a prelude to death. The camp slang for this vast majority in the Nazi camps was the *Muselmänner*—the 'walking dead'. In old Soviet camps the same corpus of hopeless people was to be found, known by a nick-name of very similar meaning, the *Dokhodyaga*—the 'goners'.

> Their life is short, but their numbers are endless: they, the *Muselmänner*, the drowned, form the backbone of the camp, an anonymous mass, continually renewed and always identical, of non-men who march and labour in silence, the divine spark dead within them, already too empty to really suffer. One hesitates to call them living; one hesitates to call their death death.
>
> (From Levi, P. *If This is a Man*, 1979.[9])

Survivors, on the other hand, were an active group of people who refused to be paralysed by a denial of what was taking place. Des Pres insists it was not hope that kept them alive. Too much hope led to despair and you were better off forgetting there was an outside world, not thinking about release, and working to achieve a moral identity of some kind that could be applied and acted on even in this most limiting of environments:

> The survivor is the figure who emerges from all those who fought for life in the concentration camps, and the most significant fact about their struggle is that it depended on fixed activities: on forms of social bondings and interchange, on collective resistance, on keeping dignity and moral sense alive.
>
> (From Des Pres, T. *The Survivors*, 1976.[4])

While the stressful situations that have been studied systematically by psychologists and other scientists are nowhere near as extreme as these, there are some intriguing parallels between the documentary evidence of those writing about camp life and the harder evidence of modern scientific research. Some of the conclusions drawn from studies of ordinary forms of stress, and of personality and coping, are extraordinarily close to those just discussed. For example, Shirley Fisher has this to say in summing up the findings from her work on homesickness among boarding school pupils: 'The vulnerable individual is the one who fails to engage the challenge offered by the new environment.'[10] Old-style boarding school regimes of the *Tom Brown's Schooldays* variety—now mercifully all but extinct—bore more than a superficial resemblance to the conditions of the camps. Psychological research, as we shall see, also highlights the same aspects of personality as destructive or constructive, and leads us to the conclusion that it is not so much the nature or even the intensity of a trauma that determines whether or not a person becomes ill—it is how the person copes with it.

MODERN RESEARCH ON STRESSFUL LIFE EVENTS

A powerful literature has grown up connecting illness with a variety of ordinary life stresses—things like bereavement, divorce and the loss of one's job. Here is one area of research where it will never be possible to carry out an intervention study—we cannot artificially create or prevent situations that have a profound impact on people's lives for the sake of research. Scientifically this presents a serious difficulty. Serious, but not insurmountable: what we can do is approach the issue from many different angles and piece together a kind of scientific jig-saw of the individual faced with challenging events in his or her life. In fact the jig-saw has come quite a long way in the past ten to fifteen years, and some of its more major sections will be explored in the remainder of this chapter.

A letter to *The Lancet* describes the mysterious circumstances of the death of a woman with anorexia:

A 32-year-old woman with a 6-year history of anorexia had been treated by psychotherapy and drugs for 18 months without success. She then failed to attend the clinic for six months until she was brought in by her mother because of severe weight loss and depression.

The mother told us that her daughter had attempted suicide by stabbing herself in the heart (a chest scar over the heart was noted). She was admitted, having lost 30% of her body weight. She refused to be fed and we started total parenteral nutrition (drip feed). After a month she was still refusing all oral feeding. We decided to try enteral feeding and a nasogastric tube was passed, against the patient's wishes and with accompanying threats from the patient that she would die if the tube was kept in place. Following placement of the nasogastric tube, she became totally mute, progressively unaware of her surroundings, and unresponsive to all stimuli—and within two hours she was dead. No cause of death was found at necropsy.

The course of the anorexia in this patient was unusual because of the suicide attempt and her assertion that she would die if a nasogastric tube was inserted. This case suggests the possibility that psychological factors may cause death—ie, our patient's behaviour resembled suicide. We cannot explain the fatal outcome in this case. Perhaps the message is that doctors should not insist on a therapeutic manoeuvre if the patient does not agree to it (!). (Exclamation mark mine!)[11]

This kind of event, mysterious as it sounds, is not uncommon in medical and psychiatric practice. Psychological influences over life and death can work in the reverse direction too: certain situations seem to be able to postpone or even prevent death. For example, a report was published, also in the *Lancet*, entitled 'Death takes a holiday: mortality surrounding major social occasions.' This study showed that the death rate among Jewish Americans declines to a lower than expected rate during the week leading up to Passover, and is higher than expected in the week after. Psychological factors appeared best able to explain this finding.[12] The same dip-rise in death rate has been noticed before and after birthdays, and a drop in death rate of American citizens is to be seen just before presidential elections.[13]

The potential for stress to act in such a way that the brain effectively dictates life or death has been suspected for a long time. Only recently, however, has it been the subject of intensive research.

Marriage

For a long time it has been known that married people are healthier, mentally and physically, than single people. The risk of death from all causes is lower at any given age if you are married. The difference is most marked when married people are compared to widowed or divorced people but it also holds true for comparisons with single people who have never married.[14]

One explanation for this is that individuals who are fit and healthy make more attractive potential partners than those who are weak and sickly. Selection of this kind will clearly work in favour of a strong species based on a strong gene pool, but we hardly need Darwin to tell us that people are drawn to health and beauty: our movie idols are proof enough of that.

A marriage, or for that matter any intimate relationship, at its best provides physical and psychological security to both partners. One might surmise that this in itself has a health-protecting quality, especially in times of difficulty. If there is someone around in whom one can confide and whose advice one can seek, then the burden is lightened.

All this may seem fairly obvious. But psychologists like to delve into such things and prove them and, sure enough, evidence for the health-protecting qualities of a good relationship is strong. George Brown's painstaking study in 1969–70 of working-class women in the urban suburb of Camberwell, London, is one of the many pieces of research that show this. The study was not specifically concerned with marriage, but it showed that in this problem-ridden community, where the rate of psychiatric illness was high, having an intimate friend—someone to trust and confide in—greatly reduced the likelihood of breaking down in the event of a crisis. This was especially so when the someone was a husband.[15]

Separation and divorce

Data from research also clearly show that divorced people suffer more physical and mental ill-health than married or single people. Getting divorced increases a person's risk of being admitted to a mental hospital more than five times. Perhaps surprisingly, the data also show a greater decline in the health of men than women following divorce. This is also the case following the death of one or other partner. Men seem less able to cope with life on their own and are more likely than women to re-marry. Each case is of course different and unique, but it has been said that women and men tend to cope with separation in different ways. Divorced men often experience an initial sense of freedom and elation and temporarily enjoy a busy social life. But after a while—anything from six months to two years—they start to feel depressed and apathetic and begin to hanker after a stable relationship again. It has been suggested that a lot of men only appreciate the good things about marriage when they no longer have them. Women, on the other hand, tend to experience depression more acutely following separation but are often able to adjust better, given time, as they get used to being on their own.[14]

From a researcher's point of view, however, the value of

looking at the effects on health of separation and divorce is rather limited. A relationship about to be dissolved is likely to have had a stormy history, so that the end of it may mark an overall reduction in the level of stress. Studies of divorced people run into the extra difficulty that physical separation of married couples often happens long before the slow legal proceedings of divorce are brought to a conclusion, and it hardly needs stating that many divorces come about because one partner meets someone else. Studying the effects of divorce on health is complicated and unsatisfactory in several respects.

Bereavement

Studying the effects of bereavement is less ambiguous. Death guarantees that even the best marriages come to an end sooner or later. Studies and statistics confirm that the psychological and physiological consequences of losing a partner are indeed profound: the risk of psychiatric illness, physical illness and death are all greatly increased in both widows and widowers (in England in the seventeenth century 'griefe' appeared on death certificates as an accredited cause of death).[13,16,17] Murray Parkes is generally regarded as the person who pioneered research in this area. In 1969 Parkes and his colleagues[18] provided scientific backing to the old death-from-a-broken-heart folklore by recording a significant increase in cardiovascular deaths in 4,500 widowers during the period following the wife's death. Studies of sudden death—that is, death, usually of cardiovascular origin, not preceded by any warning symptoms—have also shown a high incidence of fatal illness in people throughout the six months after the death of their partner.[19]

Again, men seem more vulnerable than women, especially when young. Widowed males, aged between 20 and 24, are 17 times more likely to die than their married counterparts. Widowed females in this age bracket are ten times more likely to die than married females. Men may do worse, but the chance of dying shoots up dramatically for both sexes in the first six months after the spouse's death, especially in this young age group. With increased age this very high elevation in death rate among the newly bereaved declines, but the relation between bereavement and mortality of the survivor is still there.[13]

These statistics were calculated from the Population Census for England and Wales in 1974. But there are many more calculations based on other populations and all of them confirm the same pattern: an effect on health and survival of loss for both sexes, and this most pronounced in young males and strongest in the first six months following a bereavement but still visible two and sometimes three years later.[13]

Causes of death in the newly bereaved

What are the illnesses that strike recently bereaved people and so often result in their death? Some good and very revealing figures are available on this question. Table 2 is based on data for the entire United States white population for the 1959–61 period. It shows the ratios of causes of death among widows and widowers compared to their married counterparts. So, for example, the figure 2.69 at the top left of the Table means that widowers are 2.69 times more likely than married men to die as a result of homicide attacks (deaths by violence), and 2.24 times more likely to die of liver cirrhosis . . . and so on.

There is probably some interaction between the items in Table 2, especially where alcohol is concerned. A person is in more danger of getting into a fight or having an accident when drunk; and of course very heavy drinking is known to lead to liver cirrhosis and to some gut cancers.

Table 2 is concerned with *ratios*, not with overall numbers. The three *leading* killers for all widowed people are the same as those for married people—heart disease, stroke and cancer. Although the risk of heart disease and stroke is raised only about one and a half times for widows and

TABLE 2*

Mortality ratios for widowed to married people: USA white population, 1959–1961

Widowers		Widows	
Homicide	2.69	Non-motor accidents	1.84
Liver cirrhosis	2.42	Suicide	1.66
Suicide	2.39	Heart disease	1.48
Accidents (non-motor)	2.27	Strokes	1.47
Tuberculosis	2.17	Tuberculosis	1.43
Accidents (motor)	1.99	Liver cirrhosis	1.31
Strokes	1.50	Homicide	1.28
Heart disease	1.46	Gut cancers	1.23
Diabetes	1.41	Cervical cancer	1.18
Gut cancers	1.26	Lung cancer	1.18
Lung cancer	1.26.		

*Source: National Centre for Health Statistics (1970) Series 20, No. 8. Mortality from Selected Causes by Marital Status. Government Printing Office, Washington DC.

widowers, these are the most common causes of death because they account for some 50 per cent of deaths in the married population. For every two married people who die of heart attacks and strokes, three bereaved people die from these causes.

Table 2 broadly concurs with other studies, including those of recently bereaved people, although the latter show that heart disease plays a more prominent part in the early days following a loss. The Table is especially interesting because it shows that the increase in deaths among bereaved people rests *both* on things caused by an internal organic pathology—things that are involuntary like heart disease and cancer—*and* on things that are ostensibly under the conscious control of the individual, like heavy drinking, associated with cirrhosis and suicide. We might list the causes of death in Table 2 again, according to whether they are voluntary or involuntary:

Voluntary	Involuntary
Cirrhosis (via drinking)	Heart disease
Suicide	Strokes
	Cancer
	Tuberculosis
	Diabetes

Note that I have omitted accidents and homicide from this re-classification. Under which heading should they appear? I suggest that the answer is not altogether clear. Certainly some killings are the result of provocation. If a man gets into a fight it is sometimes by choice, or if he does so because he is drunk, then, arguably, there is some choice about whether or not to get drunk in the first place. Similarly, victims of accidents are perhaps not always as careful and vigilant as they might be.

Freud was one of the first to explore the faintly sinister possibility that the victims of accidents are not always the passive recipients of fate but sometimes themselves play a part in the cause of the accidents. In his book, *The Psychopathology of Everyday Life*,[20] he suggested that accidents may be unconsciously precipitated. The pedestrian crossing the road genuinely may not *see* the car approaching. Freud argues that the not-seeing in this circumstance is not exactly deliberate but may be worked out by the individual at a level below that of conscious awareness—in other words, he unconsciously 'registers' the approaching car but represses this information so that it does not enter his consciousness. A book by Tabachnick, *Accident or Suicide? Destruction by Automobile*,[21] raises similar issues and catalogues an impressive series of findings supporting the idea of accident-proneness: that there are particular categories of people who are more likely than others to become the victims of accidents. Perhaps recently bereaved people represent one such category. There is a suggestion that unemployed people may represent another. During periods of high unemployment, such as the great depression of the 1930s, there is an overall increase in accidents of all kinds. Interestingly, there is also a synchronous increase in suicides and homicides. In fact, taking all the death statistics available in the United States from 1900 through to 1975 (which from 1933 to 1975 include records for the entire population), we find that mortality rates from suicide, homicides and motor accidents parallel one another very closely over time: when the suicide rate rises, so does the rate of dying from accidents or as a result of violence. Similarly, when the suicide rate goes down, as it did for example during the Second World War, so does the rate of fatal accidents and deaths through violence (ignoring those due to the war itself).[22]

So maybe there is little to be gained in dividing up causes of death into 'voluntary' and 'involuntary'. Maybe there is really only one category that is neither exactly voluntary nor exactly involuntary. After all, it is quite appropriate to talk about someone as 'driven' to suicide, or to drink.

These observations come close to the heart of the stress-illness hypothesis: that there is an essential relationship between a person's psychological well-being and his or her physical health and potential for survival, and that this relation is a primary one and supersedes external physical influences barring catastrophes. The various threats to life that are reliably found following the loss of one's partner —that most stressful of natural life events—do not discriminate between voluntary and involuntary, or psychological and organic, causes of death. Here is an important clue in the quest to define stress and its relation to illness.

Nevertheless, most bereaved people do not fall ill and die. So what distinguishes those who do from those who don't? Everyone who has lost someone very close must work through a difficult and often painful period of mourning. Grief is a deep-seated, natural, biologically based business and every culture has evolved rites and rituals of some kind to embrace it and give it meaning. Some psychologists have expressed concern that the sanitised, abbreviated ceremonies to despatch the dead, which have become normal practice in the West, are poor substitutes for older, more elaborate and personal proceedings. Most of the burden of consoling the survivor now falls on the support provided by family and close friends.

The question of what it is that the sick and the non-survivors suffer that the survivors do not is a crucial one for the stress-illness issue. The loss, in and of itself, cannot be the key factor since most people come through it. Are the survivors—the majority—just shallower and more thick-skinned? Is there something over-intimate and unbalanced about those partnerships in which one person cannot survive without the other? Do survivors have more friends to help them? Are they more outgoing?

The blocked action theory

Many authors have reported a pervading sense of hope-lessness as typical of those most at risk following a bereavement.[23] Others have pointed to a 'loss of security',[24] 'difficulty in adjusting',[25] a 'lack of coherence', 'helplessness',[26] an 'erosion of self-esteem',[27] a lack of 'biosocial resonation'.[28] Different theories about loss and illness use different terminologies, but often they are saying roughly the same thing. Losing a partner is losing an important source of opportunity for activity and expression: what is at risk is the sense of personhood and self-esteem that comes through action, reaction and expressive projects.

Partners offer one another many things: physical help and comfort, emotional support, advice, company and sex. However the various theories of helplessness and blocked action are all, in their different ways, saying that something more fundamental than any of these is at stake in the relation between loss, stress and illness: the inability to initiate and carry through actions in the absence of the lost person. Actions 'cannot be completed because completion would require some action or reaction from the lost partner.'[29] A state of apathy, an inability to initiate actions, is one of the most significant signs in the diagnosis of clinical depression. Depression is known to be accompanied by undesirable chemical changes in the immune system and is itself correlated with increased risk of many physical illnesses.

The blocked action theory predicts two kinds of survivor following a traumatic bereavement: 1) those able to adapt to the loss by establishing new bases for action and self-expression, and 2) those for whom the trauma of the loss is cushioned by pre-existing contacts and commitments that do not require the lost partner. These enable some continuity in the bereaved person's life. In everyday life, survival is the norm because the conditions of 1) and 2) are rich. In the Nazi camps, failure to survive was the norm because the conditions of 2) were nil—no one could carry on as they were; and the conditions of 1) were virtually nil. As we have seen, the tiny minority that managed to survive did so by virtue of 1).

Job loss and unemployment

If personal agency and self-expression, bringing a sense of self-worth, are the keys to coping with stressful life events, we would expect unfavourable effects on a person's health due to enforced redundancy and unemployment.

The rising trend in unemployment over the past two decades has seen a surge of interest in this issue and there is a considerable literature on the subject. It is virtually undisputed that unemployment is statistically associated with psychological problems, poor physical health and increased mortality from all causes.[30-33]

As usual, we must be careful in interpreting these associations and there are two points in particular that must be considered: 1) people may be less successful candidates for jobs *because* they are sick or of a sickly disposition; and 2) there is a known relation between poverty, social class and illness that exists independently of any effect of stress on health. Middle-class people enjoy better employment, a better standard of living and better all-round health than working-class people.

Happily, enough good and sufficiently detailed research on the effects of unemployment exists to help disentangle these various explanations. The evidence supports the commonsense idea that people become unemployed as a result of poor health. However, it also shows that people made redundant through no fault of their own suffer poor health compared to others of a similar age who remain in work. A typical study compared the health of 85 employees of a Norwegian sardine factory which was forced to close, with that of 85 age-matched employees of a nearby sister factory which continued to operate. Health over a four-year period was significantly worse among ex-employees.[34] Such a difference cannot be due to any selection of more healthy candidates into employment.

Two major British surveys of unemployed men, one carried out in the 1970s and one in the 1980s, give clear support to the hypothesis that raised mortality is a consequence of unemployment.[35] Both were concerned with the health of unemployed men who were actively seeking work. More people were affected by unemployment in the 1980s than in the 1970s because fewer jobs were available in the second decade. Nonetheless, similar associations between unemployment and mortality were found in both samples—again suggesting that an explanation of this relationship is to be found elsewhere than in the quality of the unemployed themselves. Moreover, the relation between unemployment and mortality held up across social classes, regions of residence and marital status, making it unlikely that any association is due to the initial poor health of the unemployed men.

There remains the possibility that lack of income on its own accounts for the unfavourable psychological and physical consequences of unemployment. Perhaps all this

TABLE 3*

Mortality ratios for unemployed to employed people: British Census of
men seeking work in 1981 and 1971

	Deaths in 1983	Deaths in 1974–81
Suicide	2.41	2.73
Accidents, poisonings and violence	2.40	2.13
Lung cancer	2.09	1.74
Ischaemic heart disease	1.82	1.20
Circulatory diseases (strokes etc.)	1.59	1.21
Other cancers	1.38	1.41
Respiratory diseases	(*insufficient number*)	1.65

*Source: Moser, K. A., Goldblatt, P. O. *et al*. Unemployment and
mortality: comparison of the 1971 and 1981 longitudinal census
samples. *British Medical Journal*, 1987, 294.

is due to an inferior diet and a less healthy physical lifestyle
among the unemployed. To investigate this we might look
at the causes of raised mortality in people out of work.
Taking the statistics from the most recent of the two British
studies, based on 14,675 men of working age who were
looking for work at the time of the 1981 Census, the raised
risk of death in this sample over the subsequent three years
is given, according to cause of death, in Table 3.

Table 3 is like Table 2—the numbers in it are *ratios* of
causes of death among unemployed men compared with
their employed counterparts. It can be seen at a glance how
strikingly similar the causes of these higher death rates are
to those in Table 2 relating to widowers. Even the ratios are
almost identical. Few of them have any obvious connection
with physical habits such as diet.

Notice particularly the appearance of more or less the
same causes of death as those in men who had lost their
wives—the same mixture, some with an obvious psychological involvement like suicide, and some straight physical

diseases like heart disease and cancer. As is the case for widowers, most unemployed people die of heart disease and cancer because these are the main causes of death in the general population.

Why should we find an almost identical list of causes of higher death rates in unemployed men looking for jobs, and almost identical proportions, as that in a totally different piece of research, carried out at a different time, in men who had lost their wives? The pattern of these findings is so symmetrical it is hard to avoid the conclusion that something very similar is going on in each instance.

Why does unemployment result in psychological distress and illness?

Loss of an income and material hardship undeniably take their toll on a person's peace of mind. Wealth may not always bring happiness but it does sweep away those everyday worries about how to pay the bills.

Modern industrial countries have systems of social security so that the grinding poverty, the malnutrition, and the insanitary conditions that the underprivileged of previous centuries had to endure have been largely eliminated. Many of today's unemployed receive redundancy payments. But cash does not seem to give protection against psychological distress, depression, and a higher rate of both mental and physical illness than that among their contemporaries who are still in work. Studies of unemployed people have revealed a threat beyond that posed by simple material deprivation. And whatever it is, its effects are often profound and can lead to the destruction of the person at his or her own hand, through misadventure, or through challenge in the form of illness.

Not always is unemployment regarded as unwelcome. In some cases unemployed men and women relish their new leisure and take the opportunity to enjoy activities and fulfil ambitions that full-time employment made impossible. But one requires resources and cash for this, and the general profile is one of apathy, low self-esteem and depression

There are a number of theories about the psychological effects of unemployment on people; that of Marie Jahoda at present dominating the academic scene.[36] Jahoda regards employment as a social institution which, besides the obvious economic benefits to the individual, has a number of latent benefits—six, to be precise. These are: time structure, social contact, activity, status, purposefulness and control. 'Benefits' may be too weak a word here. The evidence reviewed in this chapter, not only in connection with job loss, but also in relation to bereavement, and the poignant accounts of life in the concentration camps of Europe, indicates that some kind of social identity, established and fuelled through a constant programme of planned action—some kind of definite, abiding commitment—is *necessary* to psychological welfare and physical health.

An approach with a slightly different emphasis from that of Jahoda is adopted by David Fryer.[33] Fryer maintains that the most destructive component of unemployment is the restriction it imposes on the individual in terms of opportunities for doing things. He calls this the 'agency restriction' theory. In the unemployed, choices are severely limited, life is full of bureaucracy and empty of imagination. Fryer's approach differs from Jahoda's in its emphasis on the restricting effect of relative poverty on a person's life, which is seen as the principal culprit. Jahoda, on the other hand, sees the destructive consequences of unemployment persisting, even in circumstances where there are no money problems.

Though they have slightly different emphases, these, and other theories of unemployment, are similar in essence; they all see in unemployment the constriction of opportunities for action, for motivation and for meaningful commitment. Those who fail to adapt and cope by finding alternative sources suffer deep-seated feelings of worthlessness and depression. They too are the victims of blocked action as this was discussed in relation to bereavement. Coping depends upon the same two conditions as were set out in this context (p. 111).

Most studies of unemployment have focused on men. The small literature there is concerning women indicates that married and single women living in deprived environments suffer similar if not worse distress than men when they lose their jobs, this being most acute among single women.

Several enlightened investigators, including Marie Jahoda, have tried to counter the adverse effects of unemployment by setting up community-based projects of various kinds. Informal reports of the people involved in these projects are encouraging: the projects are beginning to achieve a reputation for lifting people out of apathy and depression. Unfortunately no formal study has yet been done on the effect of such interventions on people's health.

SUMMARY: PERSON AND ENVIRONMENT

In this chapter we have looked at two common life events, bereavement and job loss, which pose a challenge to the individual. Sometimes the challenge proves too great to resist and illness and even death may be the result. In the previous chapter we looked at some personality characteristics that make people susceptible to illness. The nature of the stress and the way the person copes with it, or fails to cope, combine to determine the outcome. We cannot look at person or environment in isolation: the two are constantly interacting in a dynamic way. Only in highly contrived environments such as that of the concentration camps were conditions effectively the same for everyone. Artificial though this environment was, it represents the epitome of stress, and the way some people coped gives us a profound insight into the nature of human adaptation. So severe were conditions that the great majority of prisoners broke down and became the depressed, the *Muselmänner*. This contrasts with the natural circumstances of bereavement and job loss, where most people do cope and come through, but the mechanism of coping in all three cases is strikingly similar.

The message we get is really quite a clear one. Coping with traumatic change necessitates active adjustment on the part of the individual, and this means the establishment of goals and projects that have meaning and application in the new environment and are not fossilised in the past. It was no use brooding too much about the outside world when you were incarcerated in a concentration camp. The survivors were those who quickly took stock of camp conditions and worked out their own moral programme, however difficult and tenuous this was. Coping with a bereavement or a redundancy involves similar tactics, albeit not so extreme. New plans and goals must be substituted for old ones, and they must be plans and goals that hold meaning and value. Exactly what are the origins of 'meaning' and 'value' will be explored in the following chapters.

Most people engaged in contemporary research on stress and illness take this model—of the individual in dynamic interaction with the environment—as their point of departure. Stress is the result of traumatic change which challenges psychological resources. It is easy to see that the two personality traits examined in the previous chapter are not useful assets at such times: both entail a certain psychological inflexibility. It does not help to repress the awfulness of a situation and to pretend to oneself that it's all right really, because the need to adjust, change and form new plans will not make itself sufficiently apparent. Similarly, the rigid, bulldozing, hostile single-mindedness of the Type-A person represents a distinct disadvantage in circumstances that require cool reassessment, imagination, the weighing of alternative possibilities and preparation for personal change.

Every culture has its ways of helping and supporting the individual in times of traumatic change, from institutionalised rituals like funerals to the personal help and support that friends and families give to one another. The effect of these systems of support runs deep, psychologically and physically, and will be discussed in Chapter 6. For the moment, however, we turn to the question, how is psychological stress translated into the organic states which can be so damaging to health?

Chapter 5

STRESS, THE BODY AND THE IMMUNE SYSTEM

What happens to the chemistry of the body when a person is depressed or unable to cope with stress? How does stress exert its harmful and sometimes fatal influence?

These are questions of central importance to our understanding of the relation between stress and illness. The last ten years has seen a great surge of interest in the biochemistry of stress and there have been some major discoveries, especially in regard to the effects stress can have on the immune system.

THE IMMUNE SYSTEM

The human immune system is not located in any particular part of the body but is distributed throughout it to involve virtually all of its organs. It is fundamentally a system of defence against foreign material, and its function hangs on an ability to distinguish *self* from *non-self*. This is why drugs have to be used to suppress it after organ transplant surgery. In a healthy person, infection with a bacterium or a virus triggers a finely tuned series of steps that eventually results in the destruction and removal of the invader. It also involves a remarkable ability to recognise and tolerate the indigenous population of micro-organisms that inhabit the body and are vital to it—the gut bacterium *escherichia coli*, for example. What is more, such natural flora can only be tolerated in their rightful place. If *escherichia coli* were to invade the kidneys, perhaps as a consequence of injury or surgery, infection would result and the full resources of the immune system would be brought into play.

The immune system cannot be isolated in one part of the body because micro-organisms can attack at any point —through the lungs, through the gut or through a break in the skin anywhere on the body's surface. The response to infection has to be flexibile and mobile, so the most important weapons in the body's armoury are special cells and proteins that can move through the bloodstream to any site where they are needed and be stimulated into action there. The body's system of defences is no simple matter. It involves many different weapons and targets and many messengers, or go-betweens, which orchestrate the whole action.

Suppose someone walking on a beach steps on a piece of broken glass. The skin is broken and bacteria present on the glass pass through it. The bacteria, finding themselves in a nourishing new environment, start to grow and multiply, and this immediately triggers a defensive reaction. Histamine is released causing a relaxation of small blood vessels so that the supply of blood in the area of the cut is increased. White blood cells called phagocytes are attracted to the wound and begin to engulf and eat the bacteria. After a while they die and the debris they form is a component of pus. Other phagocytes form a cordon around the wound so as to prevent bacteria spreading beyond it to healthy tissue.

All this constitutes local inflammation. Should these reactions fail and some bacteria penetrate through local defences and enter the bloodstream, there are points in the circulation—lymph nodes—where armies of fixed, non-mobile phagocytes lie in wait to trap and destroy the bacteria.

Should this secondary action fail, another powerful system of defence is mobilised so that the body starts to produce antibodies. For many infections the production of antibodies is what finally tips the balance in the war against the invaders. Antibodies are produced by white blood cells called *B-lymphocytes* and their production is regulated by sister cells called *T-lymphocytes*. There are various types of

T-lymphocyte, the main three being *helper* cells, *suppressor* cells and *natural killer* cells. Helper and suppressor cells literally help or suppress the antibody response; the role of natural killer cells will be explained in a moment. Antibodies inactivate a circulating foreigner by attaching physically to it, and this has the effect of spotlighting it for destruction by phagocytes.

This final reaction is known as the *immune response* and it requires an extremely subtle degree of co-ordination. No immunologist would claim that this is at present fully understood. However, the discovery in recent years of substances that act as messengers in the system—*cytokines*—marks a significant breakthrough in our understanding of the immune response.

Fig. 14 is a simplified sketch of the main features of the immune response. The diagram illustrates just how complex and interdependent are the various activities on which its competence depends. It shows three types of cell, B-lymphocytes, T-lymphocytes and *macrophages*, and the interactions between them. Macrophages are mobile phagocytes. Their name comes from the Greek and means 'big eaters'. All three types of cell are made by *stem cells* in the bone marrow. T-lymphocytes spend some time maturing and being prepared for their specialised functions in the thymus—hence the 'T'. Three different families of messenger cytokines are shown in this diagram—*interferons*, *interleukins*, and *tumour necrosis factor*. Just how the delicate network of communication and feedback is co-ordinated and balanced into the pattern that constitutes the immune response is at present the subject of intense research.

What relevance has all this to stress and its effects on health? Until quite recently the answer to this question would have been (and indeed was if one asked an immunologist) 'none at all'. But it has long been known that the immune response can go wrong and can turn against the body's own tissues by making antibodies to its own cells and organs. This is referred to as *autoimmunity*. Some

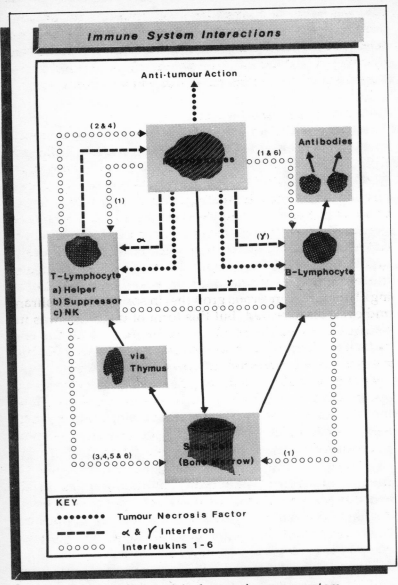

Fig. 14   The complexity of the human immune system.
These are only some of the interactions known to take
place between its cells and messengers.

diseases have for a while been believed to have an auto-immune basis, for example, rheumatoid arthritis, multiple sclerosis and pernicious anaemia. More recently it has been discovered that the immune system plays a critical part in the control of our second most common fatal illness: cancer.

Cancer and the immune system

The first scientist to suspect that the immune system is involved in the control of cancer was probably William B. Coley, a young surgeon working at Memorial Hospital in New York from 1892 to 1931. In the late nineteenth century he had some success in treating cancer patients by infecting them with both live and dead bacteria (dead ones were eventually preferred to live ones since live bacteria had an unfortunate habit of creating infections). These became known as 'Coley's toxins': it was obvious they stimulated the immune system since they provoked fever and shivering. Tumours (cancerous growths) in some patients shrank and even disappeared, but this form of treatment was not without risks and its results were haphazard. In the end, radiation therapy and chemotherapy replaced Coley's methods as the preferred ways of treating cancer.

For the next 50 years the hypothesis that the growth and spread of cancers is influenced by the immune system fell out of fashion, to such an extent that mainstream immunology—preoccupied with developing new vaccines—tended to dismiss the idea as too speculative. Then in the 1970s a substance was discovered in the blood, which seemed to have a number of important controlling roles in the immune system. One of its functions appeared to be the destruction of tumours. By the mid 1980s techniques had been developed to make this substance in sufficient quantity to enable it to be studied properly.

Tumour necrosis factor, or TNF, as it was called, was found to have both direct and indirect anti-tumour action. It damages the blood vessels that nourish a tumour, starving the tumour of oxygen and causing it to die. In addition, it stimulates T-cells and other immune mechanisms that co-operate to destroy tumours. Exactly how and in what conditions TNF destroys cancers is still not fully understood. Trials with people have shown that when it is injected directly into a tumour it can have a beneficial effect. Unfortunately it is not possible to do this with the majority of cancers.[1]

It must be remembered that the immune system is a *system*, and, as Fig. 14 shows, its effectiveness depends not on one or other element but on everything working and co-operating in concert. Treatment by upping the concentration of a single factor is rather like increasing the volume of, say, the clarinets in an orchestra a thousandfold. It may have a crude effect but it is bound to throw the whole thing out of balance: injecting people with one factor in isolation will probably turn out to have limited clinical value. Notwithstanding, for our purpose, it is sufficient to note that TNF can, directly or indirectly, destroy cancers.

Another cytokine discovered comparatively recently, *interleukin-2*, has also been found to have an anti-tumour action. Interleukin-2 acts on lymphocytes to make them grow and divide. It can transform them into 'killer cells' that recognise and destroy cancer cells. There is no doubt that interleukin-2 alone, or in combination with white blood cells, also attacks tumours and can make them shrink. Trials injecting cancer patients with combinations of cells and cytokines are currently under way.[2,3] Looking at Fig. 14, these trials still seem a relatively crude way of going about things.

Immune surveillance

As well as the action of the immune response itself, where a powerful, co-ordinated artillery is concentrated against a specific invader, or antigen, and antibodies are made in large quantity to recognise the antigen, attach to it, and so ear-mark it for destruction, there are also some non-specific weapons. Macrophages, and the dramatically named *nat-*

ural killer (NK) cells circulate in the blood and have a general policing function. They are capable of spontaneously destroying foreign matter and damaged cells without help from other sources and without an antigen being labelled by its attachment to an antibody.

Another duty of NK cells, thought to be an important one, is to destroy mutant (abnormal) and cancerous cells.[4] A number of things can cause a cell to mutate and become cancerous. Radiation is one, and there are known carcinogenic (cancer-producing) chemicals such as asbestos dust. The body makes huge numbers of replacement cells every minute. No process of copying of this order of magnitude is totally without error and calculations have been made about the likely number of faulty and mutant cells that are produced naturally. These are really no better than guesses, but it is certain that some mutant cells are naturally produced—probably in larger quantities as one gets older—and there has to be a way of removing them. The cells that police the immune system—macrophages and NK cells—are one such way. In contrast to TNF and interleukin-2, macrophages and NK cells do not seem to have much effect on established tumours. However, they can prevent tumours developing and they can stop a tumour spreading through cancerous cells detaching themselves from a primary site and travelling through the bloodstream to other parts of the body. The spreading of cancers in this way to secondary sites is common and is known as *metastasis*. But most important is whether or not a cancer starts to form in the first place and this seems to depend upon how well these cells do their job of policing.

The encouragement of cancers

We are only just beginning to unravel the sophisticated secrets of the immune system and its power to prevent and counteract cancer. To complicate matters yet further, it has recently been shown that the immune system also possesses the means for *stimulating* the growth of cancers.

Paradoxically, under some circumstances, TNF can aid cell growth, and macrophages are known to secrete substances that promote the growth of tumours.[1] It is clear that a full understanding of the human immune system will only be achieved by building up a picture of the interactions between its various constituent cells and proteins, all of which regulate one another in an extremely complicated way (Fig. 14 again).

Effects of stress on the immune system

These new discoveries strongly suggest that what often tips the balance in favour of health or ill-health is a failure of the body's own defences. A recent article in the *Lancet* was entitled: 'Is cancer a macrophage-mediated autoaggressive disease?'[5] 'Autoaggressive' means the body turning against itself. In certain instances which are at present not understood, something happens to upset the chemistry of the immune system so that cancer cells are not recognised as such and destroyed, or normal healthy tissue is wrongly identified as foreign and a hostile reaction to it is set up.

Where are we to look for the source of this disturbance? The answer, I believe, is in the psychology of the person, the situation he is in and his relation with other people. To pursue the military analogy that I have used in discussing the function of the immune system, the commander-in-chief—the ultimate overseer and balance-keeper—is the brain. Another exciting recent discovery is that the brain and the immune system enjoy a very intimate partnership.[6]

We know that stress and psychological depression have detrimental effects on the immune system—they are *immunosuppressive*, that is, they interfere with the competence and smooth-running of the system.[7,8,9] Most of the evidence for this is again fairly new and has created quite a stir, especially within immunology. This is to be expected: in the past, hard scientists have had some difficulty accepting the stress-illness hypothesis on the grounds that illness is something visible and physical, whereas stress appears too airy-fairy a concept to be scientifically creditable. But now that we are able to trace the effects of stress through to an upset in the chemistry of the immune system and resulting pathology, the grounds for this scepticism begin to evaporate.

THE EVIDENCE

The first convincing demonstration of how stress affects the competence of the immune system was a study of 26 spouses of patients who were fatally ill or who had just died from illness. Compared to 26 non-bereaved people of similar age, sex and race, the stressed group showed a significant impairment in their immune response when this was artificially challenged by the introduction of a substance that simulated an invading antigen.[10] Further studies of women undergoing major life crises, such as bereavement, found the activity of NK cells among those who were stressed to be lower than that in a comparison group of non-stressed women.[7] Moreover, NK cell activity is most impaired in those individuals who are most depressed.

Other evidence of immune deficiencies among clinically depressed and mentally ill people is now well established—'The results of these experimental and clinical studies are clear evidence that a new division of psychiatry, immunopsychiatry, has been born.'[11] Depression is a natural part of grieving, but failure eventually to come out of it and confront the changed circumstances with a new outlook is failure to cope with and adapt to the situation. We saw in the previous chapter that it is failure to *cope* with stress, rather than the presence or absence of stress itself, that results in a breakdown of health. Several studies of immune function mirror this. One study of students showed that overall life stress had no effect on NK cells, but high stress combined with poor coping and depression resulted in a substantial reduction in NK cell activity.[12]

Two studies, one of psychiatric patients and one of American medical students, are of particular interest since they both related reduced NK cell activity specifically to feelings of loneliness and social isolation.[13,14]

A tendency to repress and deny negative emotions, such as anger, is associated with a predisposition to various forms of cancer (see Chapter 3). Some recent evidence has shown the same personality traits also to be associated with decreased immune competence in the form of a reduction in the numbers of certain lymphocytes.[15]

Janice Kiecolt-Glaser and her colleagues at Ohio State University have carried out a mini-intervention study. Forty-five residents of an old people's home were taught special relaxation techniques which were presented to the residents as a way to become generally more active and involved. At the end of the training the relaxation group showed a significant increase in NK cell activity compared to a comparison group who, instead of the training, only had routine visits from students.[16]

The workings of the immune system have also been studied in the context of unemployment. Sure enough, the evidence again shows that the immune system does not function as well when you are out of work as when you are in it.[17]

Janice Kiecolt-Glaser and her team are also interested in the effects that the quality of a relationship might have on the smooth running of the immune system. They reason that if a person has a good, stable, happy relationship with his or her partner, life will be a lot easier because a good relationship is the source of numerous pleasures, and any problems and stresses that arise can be shared and worked through together. They studied the quality of the relationship in married couples as well as marriages that had broken down. Women and men whose relationships had failed, and who had separated, showed signs of depression as well as evidence of an impoverished immune response. For both sexes better marital quality was associated with less depression and a better immune response.[18,19]

Our own study of volunteers coming to Harvard Hospital, a special research unit for the common cold, at Salisbury, Wiltshire, produced findings consistent with these using a rather different approach. Volunteers came to stay at the unit for a fortnight and allowed themselves to be infected with a common cold virus. We studied 52 people. Before infecting them, they were screened for antibody level to the virus using blood samples. The dose of virus given was precisely the same for everyone—so here we have a controlled situation where people with equivalent initial immunity receive identical exposures to the same virus.

Before they were infected, various measures of recent life stress and personality were made by psychologists. Later, the severity of the cold each person developed was assessed by a medical team on the basis of symptoms and the amount of virus that was shed. More virus (heavier infection) was found in those people who had experienced most changes in their recent lives. In addition, extraversion, a measure of personality denoting sociability and expressiveness, emerged as a significant protective factor: extraverts had less severe infections than introverts (measured using the Eysenck Personality Inventory).[20]

The recent research concerned with the immune systems of people who are in stressful situations which, for one reason or another, they are unable to resolve is very important. Findings are broadly consistent and together they add up to powerful evidence both for the stress-illness hypothesis itself, and for the hypothesis that some of the effects which stress can have on health are mediated by the immune system. What finally puts the seal of authenticity on this conclusion is the fact that immune system deficits appear *proportional* to psychological distress—the more the stress, the greater the depression, the less well the immune system is able to fulfil its function—the less well, for example, NK cells seem able to carry out their duty of spontaneously removing naturally arising cancer cells.[21]

There still remains a missing link. How do the effects of stress, as it is registered by the brain and suffered by the person, make themselves felt on the immune system? Again, research on this question has come a long way in recent years.

All animals react naturally to acute threat with a series of co-ordinated, automatic, bodily changes. Most of these will be familiar: the pupils dilate, the mouth goes dry as saliva is inhibited, heart rate quickens, passages to the lungs widen, digestion and the bladder are inhibited and the liver produces glucose for energy. The reactions in this list are aided by the release of the hormone *adrenaline* into the blood by the adrenal glands.

These biological changes are adaptive: they prepare the organism for one or other of two self-protecting actions—fight or flight. In the normal course of things they might be expected to be short-lived; one or other strategy—aggression or escape—works, the threat is dealt with and the body's functions return to normal. Alternatively, the organism succumbs and dies.

Sometimes, however, especially in the complicated human world, it is not altogether possible to distance oneself from a threat in one or other of these straightforward ways and life goes on against its constant presence. This is what living under stress means and if the stress is intense enough, some of the automatic responses that are meant as an acute resource do not die away as they should but instead persist over time. Such a state of affairs, when prolonged, is clearly maladaptive. It results in damage to the thymus and the adrenal glands and it causes ulcers.

But it has other, more sinister, consequences than these. *Cortisol*, one of the products of the adrenal glands, has been shown to have a number of effects that antagonise the immune system and render it less efficient. It suppresses the activity of macrophages, it attacks T-cells and it destroys

NK cells.[22] Prolonged exposure to cortisol weakens the body's defences. Cortisol is also a reliable index of depression; indeed, so reliable that an elevated level of cortisol in the blood is often used as a tool in the diagnosis of clinical depression.[23]

The sequence of events culminating in the suppression of the immune system is as follows: a chronic stress reaction starts with a threat—conscious or unconscious—and the inability of the person to cope with it. This requires signals to the brain from sense organs and the interpretation of the meaning of these signals and their implications, all of which goes on in the higher, 'thinking' regions of the brain—the outer layer, or cerebral cortex. The cerebral cortex communicates with the limbic system and the hypothalamus —two very important centres in the mid-brain, which regulate, among many other things, memory and emotion. If it is decided that a serious threat exists, the hypothalamus releases a local messenger, *corticotropin releasing factor* (CRF), which stimulates the pituitary gland, situated nearby in the brain, to secrete a hormone, *adreno-corticotropic hormone* (ACTH), into the blood. ACTH is a long-distance messenger substance which travels through the blood to its target organ, the cortex, or outer layer, of the adrenal glands positioned near the kidneys. ACTH causes the adrenals to secrete corticosteroids into the blood. This is how the products of the stress reaction such as cortisol come into contact with cells of the immune system and interfere with their smooth functioning (see Fig. 15).

Built into this chain of causes and effects is a negative feedback loop, shown to the right of the diagram. This regulates the whole sequence and ensures it does not get out of hand. When levels of cortisol and other substances produced by the adrenal glands become too high, a signal is sent back to the hypothalamus to cut down its production of CRF. This feedback loop is of crucial importance in keeping the reaction under control. But it, too, appears to be controlled by substances produced in the brain, known as *opioid peptides*. The presence of opioid peptides encourages the inhibitory influence on the production of CRF: that is, the negative feedback loop regulating the production of CRF itself appears answerable to the influence of opioid peptides.[24]

There is yet another vehicle of self-regulation. Cells in the immune system are able to communicate back to the brain! When the resources of the immune system are mobilised to counter-attack an invader, this causes intense activity in the hypothalamus.[25]

The details of this system, like those of the immune system itself, are still nowhere near fully understood. Figs. 14 (p. 122) and 15 give a very crude picture of some of the processes involved and the complexity and delicacy of their organisation. They show how variations at any point can throw things out of balance so that the burden of restoring order is shifted one level up to a higher-order regulating mechanism. Only two levels of regulation are shown in Fig. 15—the negative feedback loop and the counter-regulation of this by opioid peptides. But it is likely that there are more hierarchical levels of control, making the entire business very complex indeed. Failure to cope with stress eventually overloads the forces working to maintain the system's equilibrium and integrity.

Fig. 15 shows how intimately the brain, the nervous system and the immune system co-operate and interact. In a sense, recent discoveries imply that it is silly to draw too sharp a distinction between the two systems. Perhaps, when more is known about their respective functions and interactions, they will be regarded as one system rather than two.[26] Not long ago this idea would have been heresy within the ranks of traditional neurology and immunology.

There are other reasons to make us think we are dealing with a single system. Bone marrow, the source of the cells and proteins that make up the immune system, is richly endowed with nerves and nerve endings. The thymus —the school for the training of many immune system

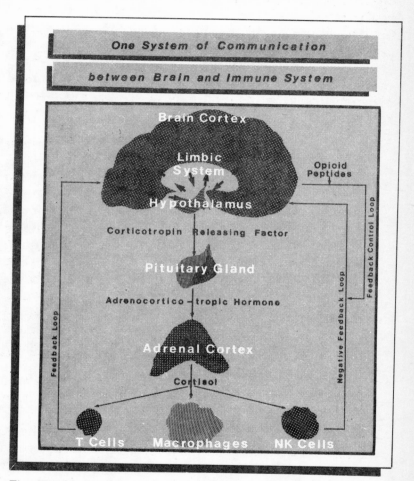

Fig. 15   The way the brain communicates stress to the rest of the body; in particular, the immune system. Note that cells in the immune system, NK cells for example, can send messages back to the brain.

recruits for their different but interrelated roles—is directly wired to the brain. So too are the lymph nodes—the centres at various sites around the body for trapping circulating undesirables (see Fig. 16). Why should this be if the brain and immune system are, as used to be thought, autonomous and independent of one another?

Recent research has also revealed special receptors, like ports, on T-cells, including NK cells, for neuropeptides —chemicals responsible for communication within the brain and central nervous system (Fig. 16).[26,27]

All in all, the case for regulation of the immune system by the brain and counter-regulation of the brain by the immune system is overwhelming. So too is the evidence that both systems respond together in times of stress. As one author puts it in a review of the field, 'Much of the work to be discussed in this paper will be based on the assumption that the body's regulatory systems do, in fact, regulate one another.'[22]

In concluding this section about the immune system, it can be said that recent research on stress, immunity and illness is forcing us to take a more holistic attitude to the physiology involved. It heavily underlines the limitations of too narrow a disciplinary focus if we are to reach a full understanding of bodily breakdown in times of stress. It makes us see the body as an *organism* as well as a collection of organs.

AIDS

The evidence building up concerning stress and the immune system brings us to ask whether stress could conceivably play a part in the development of AIDS.

AIDS (Acquired Immune Deficiency Syndrome) is basically a disorder of T-lymphocyte functioning. Victims of the disease are found to have fewer helper T-cells than is normal and of the T-cells they do have, many are defective. Recent research hints that macrophages are another

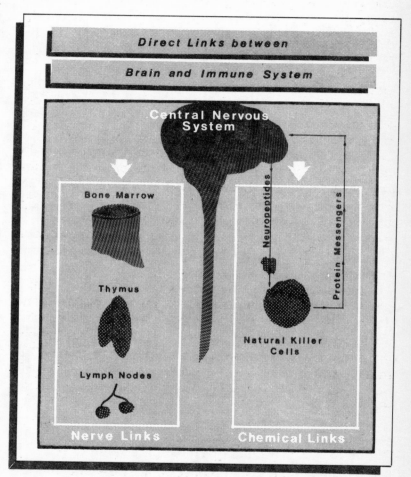

Fig. 16 Brain and immune system are intimately related. There are many points of direct, hard-wired contact (shown to the left of the diagram), as well as close chemical contact with circulating cells (shown to the right of the diagram).

target. As Fig. 14 (p. 122) shows, T-cells and macrophages are central to an effective immune response. A defective T-cell and macrophage population means a defective immune system, so that people with AIDS have a seriously flawed armoury of defences. They are easy prey to opportunistic invaders and are thus prone to viral, bacterial and fungal infections as well as to cancer. There is no standard constellation of symptoms in an AIDS sufferer—a weak immune system leaves the victim open to a wide range of serious and fatal conditions.

The changes in T-cell function are believed to be caused by a virus: HIV (human immunodeficiency virus; more technically, HTLV-III, human T-cell lymphotropic virus III). But there are a few puzzling things about the relation of the HIV virus to the condition of AIDS, which remain to be explained:

1   The virus appears to have an exceptionally long latency period—roughly five years. This is unlike any other known virus. The immune system ought to have plenty of time to eliminate it.

2   Not all patients diagnosed as having AIDS are HIV positive. Many are HIV negative. The revised guidelines of 1987, issued by the Centers for Disease Control in the United States, describe how to diagnose AIDS when the laboratory evidence for HIV is negative.

3   The virus, when present in AIDS patients, is present in extremely small quantities; so small, in fact, that even if it were to destroy the corresponding number of T-cells every 24 to 48 hours, 'it would hardly ever match or beat the natural rate of T-cell regeneration'.[28]

4   The majority of people diagnosed as HIV positive do not go on to develop AIDS. Current estimates are that something between ten and forty per cent do.

5   A few cases have been reported of patients without symptoms of AIDS, who were previously HIV positive

and then became HIV negative. Could this mean that in some circumstances the virus can be defeated?[29]

These five points suggest that the relation between HIV and AIDS is perhaps not as clear-cut as is frequently assumed. Could this be another case of too much focus on 'external' causes and not enough attention to 'internal' ones? After all, it is much simpler and much more convenient to say 'HIV is the cause of AIDS'. It makes research into the disease look more promising and fundworthy.

It certainly would appear from the above that there is plenty of scope in the development of AIDS for the influence of stress, even if stress is not itself a direct cause of the disease. Could the presence or absence of stress and the hormonal environment in the body associated with stress figure in whether a person who is HIV positive goes on to develop AIDS? Can an individual in some circumstances produce chemicals in the right quantities and the right places to kill the virus and thereby revert to normal health?

Could it be the presence of the virus *plus* stress that triggers the disease? The highest risk groups in Europe and North America are promiscuous homosexuals and drug users. Are these groups of people victims of a lot of stress? Is it conceivable that personality plays a part in who gets sick and who stays well?

These questions are at present no more than questions. Nevertheless, huge funds are poured into AIDS research; HIV has the reputation of being by far the most expensive virus ever studied. It might be worth adopting a wider perspective and taking a look at what internal bodily conditions are hostile or hospitable to the virus and its potential development into a full reaction.

HEART DISEASE AND SUDDEN DEATH

As well as suppressing the immune system, cortisol, along with other stress hormones such as noradrenaline, has various villainous effects in the arteries. It causes damage to artery walls, increases the stickiness of platelets (cells in the blood that aid blood clotting) and attracts fatty deposits in the inside lining of artery walls. In these ways it tends to further the process of atherosclerosis, conditioning the blood vessels so as to make thrombosis and heart attack that little bit more likely.[30]

But cortisol and these other hormones are not really villains in themselves. Like cholesterol they are vital substances. It is their presence in the wrong places for extended periods of time that does the damage. And this happens when a stressful situation exists and the individual fails to cope with it and resolve it.

Sudden cardiac death is the leading cause of death in industrially developed countries, and it is well known that people with atherosclerosis are at greater risk than those with healthy arteries. Nonetheless, it is not uncommon among people in whom no evidence of heart disease can be found. What is the explanation of this? There is evidence that it often happens during moments of intense emotion: overwhelming shock, panic, despair—or even excitement.

It happens on account of a disruption in the rhythm of the heart, known as *ventricular fibrillation*. The heart's normal, steady rhythm gives way to disorderly spasms—fibrillations—so that the co-ordination between its chambers is lost and blood cannot be pumped effectively. We now know that the frontal lobe of the brain is often the originator of this critical disturbance. This is the area where information is assembled about the self, the meaning and significance of events and what actions should be taken to deal with them.

Cardiac arrhythmia occurs when the normal synchronised messages to the heart are overlaid by conflicting signals. Putting it crudely, the brain appears unable to decide between two alternative strategies, so that two incompatible sets of instructions are sent to the heart muscle. There are various hypotheses about the precise nature of the ambiguity. It has been suggested that the sympathetic and parasympathetic nervous systems send competing messages.[31] The sympathetic nervous system normally mobilises the organism for fight or flight, the parasympathetic nervous system tells it to withdraw and conserve resources. The two systems are antagonistic but in the healthy person they are geared so that they function in a complementary fashion—one taking dominance over the other depending upon the situation. If messages from the brain cause both systems to be activated simultaneously, a contradictory instruction will be sent to the heart and it will perhaps be told simultaneously to speed up and slow down, or simultaneously to contract and relax.

An alternative theory has it that the confused message to the heart arises from competition, not between sympathetic and parasympatheic nervous systems, but between the right and the left hemispheres of the brain—each sending different instructions to the heart via the sympathetic nervous system.[32]

Whichever theory, or combination of theories, proves correct, evidence that cardiac arrhythmias originate in the brain is strong. Here, then, is another direct and important route by which the effects of stress can be translated into effects on health.

CONCLUSION

The aim of this chapter has been primarily to give a few key examples of some of the physiological mechanisms behind the stress-illness link, rather than to describe the immune system, the hormone system, the nervous system, and the relations between them, in any great detail. There are numerous other possible routes for the transmission of stress, which have had no mention. For example, the suggestion has been put forward that the formation of atherosclerotic plaques causing arteries to become clogged involves a deficiency in the immune system's ability to kill mutant cells from which plaque cells derive.[33] And the list of hormones that research has shown to respond to stress extends far beyond cortisol, adrenaline and noradrenaline —the examples used here.

Nevertheless, these examples are enough to show that the stress-illness hypothesis can no longer be dismissed on the grounds of 'no physiological basis'. Far from it: research has uncovered some powerful and sophisticated systems of communication, and continues to do so. What seems increasingly clear is that a proper understanding of these systems will not be achieved by studying single elements in isolation. Pumping interleukin-2 into people may have some limited clinical application in the treatment of certain cancers, but we are having to concede that giving large doses of one factor on its own is a very crude way of trying to simulate the body's natural defences, and one that has dangerous side-effects. Knowledge will only cohere when the interactions between all the various components and systems are described so that they may be represented as a single, very complex system. The question must be raised whether the traditional investigative procedures of science have the power to do this, or whether it will require a radically new methodology.[34]

Chapter 6

THE HEALTH-GIVING NATURE
OF SOCIAL SUPPORT

So far we have been concerned with situations and events in people's lives which involve traumatic change in some form—circumstances which place sudden and often un-expected demands on a person's capacity to adapt and change. It has become clear through observation and re-search that these stresses are not necessarily, on their own, injurious to health. If the person possesses the resources to cope effectively with a stressful situation, the biochemical imbalances that eventually result in damaged health, some of which were explored in the previous chapter, can be avoided. So what is the secret of successful coping? What are these mysterious resources that some people seem to have and other people lack? Are they things we can do anything about or are we all just stuck with the way we are?

There would be little point in writing a book such as this one—indeed, in doing research into stress and illness at all—if the answer to the last part of this question were 'yes'. It certainly appears true that some personalities are more prone than others to the harmful consequences of stress —the Type-A trait and the tendency to suppress negative emotions being two outstanding examples. What attempts there have been by researchers to modify these traits—for example, by giving relaxation training to Type-A people —have so far met with success (Chapter 3). Nevertheless, support for the stress-illness hypothesis and the *internal* theory of health within mainstream medicine remains thin, despite its good showing against, for instance, the diet-illness hypothesis. And mainstream medicine is where the funds are for doing research. The medical model of the body as a collection of more or less independent and specialised organs, each with its own array of controls —like sets of biochemical knobs and dials—has always been at the heart of medicine, and it is easy to see why. Knobs and dials are there to be switched and twiddled, and it is nice to think this can be done with the right drug or food regimen, or with surgical intervention. Even if we do not have all the answers at the moment, there is a powerful and largely unchallenged assumption that traditional medical methods and traditional research, founded on the ideal of specialism, will get there in the end.

The stress-illness hypothesis is based on premises that are incompatible with this: that the person is a complex single entity, that the body is a complex organism, that its organs are interdependent and that its overall integrity and health are regulated by the brain in close partnership with the endocrine system (hormones) and the immune system. This is a complete departure from the metaphysics, methods and practice of traditional medicine. It is not to say that medicine's methods are of little or no value: many preventions and interventions are self-evidently beneficial to the patient. But under the *internal* theory, medical treatments of untimely chronic degenerative illnesses are all to be seen as essentially palliative: as making the illness more bearable. It is the symptoms of these diseases that become the subject of medical treatment, not the root cause which has to do with the collapse of the integrity of the system as a whole.

What we can do to avoid stress and improve our health is of course the key question that the *internal* theory must face. There are certainly things that can be recommended at a personal level (. . . if you fit the Type-A profile, choose some form of regular relaxation training that suits you . . . etc.) and we shall return to these later. First, however, we need to deepen our understanding of the forces involved in the stress-illness relation by looking not just at the individual but at the person in the context of his or her social environment. Bereavement, the natural life event most strongly linked to illness and death, involves the loss of someone loved and valued. On the other, more positive side of the coin there is good evidence that contact with other people can often protect health, in and of itself, and also by taking the sting out of a situation that is stressful. In both cases we are concerned with bonds that exist between people. It is important to explore the nature of these bonds.

Social support

The presence of what social scientists call *social support* has been consistently linked, through research, with a low risk of numerous physical and psychiatric illnesses, and with favourable prognosis in sick patients. The absence of social support, on the other hand, is associated with poor health and poor prognosis. Social support has been studied in relation to a wide range of physical illnesses, including heart disease, cancer, hypertension and respiratory disorders, and there is good evidence that it exerts a favourable influence on health in all of these.[1-5]

Good support from family and friends can also mitigate the potentially harmful effects of stress by helping people under stress to cope better with the situation. Sometimes support can actually prevent a crisis occurring.

These statements summarise the conclusions from what is now a very sizeable literature on the role of social support. The link between social support and health has become a central theme in theories of stress and illness.

Can this link perhaps be explained on the grounds that people who are ill attract a smaller number of friends and social contracts than those who are healthy? Berkman and Syme were among the first to tackle this question. They made a study of that much studied population, the residents of Alameda County, California, over a nine-year period.[6] They found that people who initially had very poor health were indeed a little less likely than others to have friends and social contacts. However, the reverse direction of influence was much more powerful. With initial health status taken into account—that is, splitting the population into graded categories of initial poor health—people with fewer social contacts, notwithstanding how well or ill they were, still had a higher risk of illness and death than those with greater social involvement.

Alternatively, can the relationship be explained by saying that a richer social life carries with it a healthier lifestyle, in terms of things like exercise, smoking and a better use of the health services? Again the answer is no; the overall relationship between social networks and health and mortality is not adequately explained by any of these factors.

Since the Alameda County study, carried out in the 1970s, other large-scale prospective studies, in and outside America, have been completed, and the great majority of these have confirmed the relation between social support and health. Furthermore, they back Berkman and Syme's conclusion that this is neither a consequence of illness itself leading to restricted social contacts nor a result of people with lots of friends having healthier lifestyles. A random sample of the population of Sweden, numbering 17,433 men and women studied over six years, found that 'Low social support, as indicated by a relatively low level of social interaction and few social ties, was associated with an excess mortality risk of approximately 50%'.[7] The authors go on to conclude, 'Although a number of questions still remain, the present study does provide additional support for the hypothesis that there is an independent association between lack of social support and mortality. The demonstration that this association exists in the entire Swedish population strengthens the overall conclusion that social isolation has an adverse impact on health . . . social support may have the potential of increasing host resistance and of thereby improving human health and well-being.' A similar but smaller study involved 1,060 elderly Finnish men and women being followed for 6.5 years, during which time 393 people died. Its findings showed that living alone and number of social contacts did not predict survival, but 'social participation', meaning intensity of involvement with other people, did.[8] The theory that social support itself results in favourable effects on health is therefore supported by a process of elimination of other possibilities.

Although the majority of studies of social support agree in their finding of a significant relation between social support and health, agreement is not quite unanimous. For example, no connection could be found between social activities and male mortality from heart disease in a study of Japanese men living in Hawaii.[9] And in a recent study of 13,301 Finnish people, the relation was strong for men but weak and inconsistent for women.[10] These discrepancies are often put down to differences between countries in their social and cultural practices. It must be remembered, however, that in studying 17,000 or 13,000-odd people, it is not feasible to obtain anything more than an extremely rough measure of an individual's friends and contacts and the value he or she attaches to them. In the Finnish study, for example, extent of social support was assessed simply on the basis of these five questions:

1   What is your current marital status?
2   How often do you visit friends and relatives?
3   On the average, how many different homes of friends or relatives do you visit per month?
4   How many people usually come to see you or call on you per day?
5   How often do you go to meetings of clubs, associations, or societies?

The Swedish study,[7] which showed a stronger relationship between social support and health, used 18 rather than five questions as its measure of social interaction. Even 18 questions, though, seems a thin basis on which to assess so personal a thing as level of social support. Intuitively it can be argued that the quality of friendships is just as important as the number of friends a person has, maybe more so. Sure enough, when smaller numbers of people are studied, and more sensitive measures of level of social support are used—measures that take into account the meaning and depth of friendships and relationships to an individual—the relationship between social support and health is found to be consistent and strong.[11]

In one study, 208 women, all with diagnosed breast cancer, were traced over a 20-year period and their survival was successfully predicted on the basis of level of social involvement prior to their diagnosis.[12] Level of involvement here was assessed from special interviews with each person. Having regular close contact with family or friends has also been shown to predict rehabilitation in 23 patients on kidney machines.[13]

The sociologist George Brown and his colleagues undertook a painstakingly detailed study of depression among women living in deprived conditions in the London Borough of Camberwell in the 1970s. The emphasis of this study was to obtain as much detail as possible from the women about difficulties and stresses in their lives, the background to these, and about the amount and nature of support they were getting from their friends. Each person was interviewed at length and in this way data that amounted to abbreviated biographies were built up and an assessment was made not only of the specific stresses people were under and the support they were getting, but also of the meaning of this stress and the quality of support. The study showed quite clearly that having at least one close friend who was a confidant reduced the risk of serious depression by a factor of four.[14]

INTERVENTION STUDIES

A few experimental tests have been made in which support has been offered to some people but not others. A group of widows judged to be at high risk for developing symptoms because they had little support from family and friends benefited from such a programme: those who were given support had fewer physical and mental problems a year after their bereavement than those in an equivalent group who were not.[15]

The favourable effect of introducing support has been shown to carry over into labour and childbirth. First-time mothers were randomly allocated either to endure labour on their own or to receive support from an untrained woman in the form of touch, where asked for, and friendly conversation. Complications in the unsupported group were much more common than those in the supported group. Three-quarters of the mothers without support had complications—induction, foetal distress, stillbirth or Caesarian section—against only 12 per cent of those in the supported group. The length of labour was half as long in the supported group.[16]

Homes for the elderly provide a good opportunity for this kind of research: all the residents share roughly the same environment, food and lifestyle. In one Swedish study an intensive programme of social activity was introduced to one floor of an old persons' home. Music, art and other workshops were created and outings were arranged. Six months later, various physical measurements were taken and compared with similar measurements taken at the start of the study and with those of residents living on an adjacent floor. Significant improvements were found in levels of anabolic hormones (estradiol, testosterone, de-hydroepiandrosterone and growth hormone) in the intervention group. These are all hormones that tend to make for health and protect the body from the harmful effects of stress.[17]

Finally, a study that leaves no doubt at all about the power of social support over life and death was recently published in the *Lancet*.[18] This involved 86 women, all of whom were suffering from metastatic, or spreading, breast cancer. All the women were given the same medical treatment, but some of them—those who made up the intervention group—participated in specially organised weekly group meetings.

Each week for a year the women in the intervention group met for a 90-minute session led either by a psychiatrist or by a social worker. An atmosphere was created that was conducive to open discussion and the free expression of emotions. No suggestion was made that participation in the sessions would affect the course of the disease; people were simply urged to join in and talk to others about their feelings. As might be expected, strong relationships developed and a strong sense of sharing grew up among the women—'Clearly, the patients in these groups felt an intense bonding with one another and a sense of acceptance through sharing a common dilemma.'[18]

Ten years later only three of the patients were still alive. The authors of the study compared the average survival time of those who took part in the group therapy with those who did not. Survival was not good in either case, because a cancer that is spreading represents an advanced state of the disease. The average survival time of those not given group therapy was 18.9 months; that of those given the therapy, 36.6 months. So meeting and talking once a week over the course of one year effectively doubled life expectancy. This difference is highly significant, both in the technical statistical sense, and in its demonstration of the profound influence a person's involvement with others has over health and survival.

THE NATURE OF SOCIAL SUPPORT

Given the strong evidence that social support protects health, what exactly is social support and how does its protective effect work? The concept has shown itself to be of great interest to several groups of professionals—social workers, nurses and psychiatrists, as well as academic psychologists, sociologists and anthropologists. There is no universally agreed formal definition of the term. Authors of studies have different ideas about the vital ingredient of social support and these differences are naturally reflected in the way level of support is measured: the literature contains not one but many definitions. Those in the caring professions emphasise the importance of the physical and instrumental aid that friends can provide. Biologists emphasise the practical advantages for survival of attachments and mutual collaboration. Those with a more psychological or psychiatric bent place importance on the emotional support family and friends provide in times of stress; friends can help strengthen a person's defences by saying things that boost confidence and by giving moral encouragement.

Sociologists have pointed to the importance of the social network as a provider of information. Embodied in any society or group of people is a set of rules for normal and morally proper behaviour and a system of roles defining everyone's place in the scheme. Insofar as the individual has good access to this information through social contacts (sociologists call this 'social integration'), he or she is protected from uncertainty and has the confidence to assess situations accurately, make the correct decisions and so act appropriately and effectively. Whereas 'emotional support' has to do with justifying an individual's thoughts and actions and helping him avoid anxiety and guilt, support as the provision of information refers to a person's understanding of the rites and rituals of the social world.

In fact these different approaches are a good deal more intertwined and overlapping than I have made them seem. Modern discussions of social support acknowledge its many-sided nature and treat the different approaches as complementary rather than competing.[19] The differences in emphasis have resulted in different ways of assessing social support in research and it is all the more impressive, considering there is no common theoretical base, that

studies do show such good overall agreement. The literature is full of affirmations of the finding that people who are
well supported have a better chance of staying alive and
healthy than those who lack support. There is some evidence to suggest social support may be of particular benefit
to Type-A persons.[20]

Rural cultures with long-standing traditions might well
react with incredulity to our Western need to demonstrate
and prove this fact through scientific research. Anthropological accounts of such cultures tell us that often no sharp
distinction is drawn between the quality of a person's
relations with others and their physical and mental state of
health. An interesting example is provided by the concept
of *pena*, meaning sadness or suffering, which occupies a
central position in the daily discourse of Quecha-speaking
communities in highland Ecuador. The theme of social
reciprocity is strong among the Quechas: rituals serving to
mark and sustain it take up a considerable amount of the
daily routine. *Pena* is a condition afflicting people in whom
the ideal of reciprocity has broken down: sufferers become
apathetic and withdrawn and enter a state not unlike what
we would call clinical depression. If it is not resolved *pena*
leads on to a variety of physical symptoms including vomit-
ing, diarrhoea and heart pain, and then to more serious
conditions. To prevent this happening strong efforts are
made by the family and friends of the victim to step up
social contact and restore the quality and balance of the
relationships between the individual and other people,
which are considered so important to health.[21] The belief
that a person's health depends upon a harmony between
the person and the community is very common in primitive
societies, and theories of health and healing are often
organised around this theme.[22]

Institutions of social support in the modern world

Theory behind the social support-illness hypothesis is un-
tidy, as we have seen. Nonetheless there is clearly a power-

ful force at work here. Physically being with other people can help in obvious co-operative ways, but 'social support' implies something beyond this. Human beings are thinking, remembering and imagining animals. Whether someone is well supported or not must be regarded as a state of mind that is carried forward from actual physical encounters with others into the rest of the person's life. Antonovsky has tried to capture the essence of this in his idea of a 'sense of coherence'.[23] The sense of coherence is a sort of permanent mental attitude and is defined as 'a global orientation that expresses the extent to which one has a pervasive, enduring though dynamic feeling of confidence that one's internal and external environments are predictable and that there is a high probability that things will work out as well as can be reasonably expected.' But this is not quite enough. We are left wondering where the sense of coherence comes from and exactly what is its nature.

Rites and rituals for the expression of social support are not the exclusive property of primitive cultures. In the modern developed world the family may no longer be the pivotal basis of social interaction that it once was, but it is far from extinct and its influence can still be potent. Lack of cohesion and an absence of positive attitudes between family members has been related to enhanced risk of several illnesses, among them, heart disease and cancer.[24–26] There have even been moves in social medicine to urge practitioners to take the family itself as the unit for diagnosis and treatment rather than treating individual members separately.[27]

Small work groups are a little like families. In an interesting but neglected study of small groups of shift workers, Cassel recorded higher levels of serum cholesterol in men working on shifts whose personnel varied than in men whose shifts always included the same group of people.[28]

'Family' is a metaphor favoured by religious orders to describe their membership. Belonging to a religious community offers the individual a powerful source of social support through opportunities to meet regularly, the sharing of commitments and beliefs and their expression in the established rituals and liturgies that lie at the heart of all faiths. But the psychology of religion goes deeper than this. The emotional support that religious orders are able to offer is nowhere more openly on display than at revivalist meetings where a charismatic leader inducts frenzied novices into the Faith. The tears, the trances, the embraces, show that emotions run very high on these occasions. Something important is on offer—the psychological security and intimacy that comes with a sense of belonging.

As might be expected on the support-illness hypothesis, people holding religious beliefs and regular church-goers enjoy better health than non-believers and non-attenders. Hypertension, heart disease, cervical cancer, cancer of the rectum, tuberculosis, emphysema and cirrhosis of the liver are all conditions that have been documented as less frequent among those in the former categories.[29-31] A number of differences in lifestyle certainly account for some of these differences in health. The overall lower rate of smoking in religious groups protects against lung cancer; the overall lower rate of drinking, against cirrhosis and some other complaints. But when these differences in physical habit are taken into account, active religious groups still enjoy better general health: the stronger the commitment, the better health is found to be.

The most powerful protective factor here again is probably the current of social support that flows in these communities. An extreme example of this is seen in close-knit, isolated religious groups. In Chapter 2, a study was mentioned which showed the blood pressure of a secluded group of Italian nuns who observed the vow of silence, to have remained stable over a 20-year period, despite a diet high in salt, while that of a group of women in a nearby village, who were not insulated from the gathering momentum of economic change, rose over the same period.[32] As we saw in Chapter 1, the low rate of heart disease and cancer among Seventh Day Adventists has often in the past been attributed to their vegetarian diet, yet Mormons too have a low rate of these illnesses although they eat meat and dairy products.

It is often difficult in this kind of research to rule out alternative (non-psychological) explanations. Some have been positively confirmed. Economic modernisation is indeed correlated with increase in body weight and alcohol consumption, and both these contribute to various diseases. But evidence has it that the stress of cultural change *per se*—the breaking up of traditional customs and the undermining of long-held beliefs—poses a threat to health. The classic summing-up remarks of Henry and Cassel in 1969, arrived at from a systematic review of 18 world-wide studies of blood pressure levels in different cultural groups, have been reinforced by the research that has been done since. Henry and Cassel concluded that in general, blood pressure levels are healthier where the culture is stable, traditional forms are honoured and the members of the group are well adapted to them from an early age.[33]

The conclusion reached by Henry and Cassel is strikingly similar to that of Leaf, who was interested in longevity and who made a study of remote, isolated rural communities where the people lived to a great age and were comparatively free of illness. Leaf remarks, 'It is characteristic of each of the areas I visited that the old people continue to be contributing, productive members of their society. The economy in all three areas is agrarian, there is no fixed retirement age and the elderly make themselves useful doing many necessary tasks around the farm or the home . . . People who no longer have a necessary role to play in the social and economic life of their society generally deteriorate rapidly.'[34]

Support in times of stress

Apart from the protective shield that good quality social support supplies, it is generally accepted that it can also have the effect of buffering stress in times of major life change.

Studies of immigrant communities have sometimes thrown up difficulties for the stress-illness hypothesis. Moving to another country involves a certain amount of stress, it would seem, in that it requires fairly wide-ranging adaptation. One would expect the health of immigrants, on average, at least in the first years of settling, to be worse than that of the indigenous population. Generally this is found to be so,[35] but it is not always the case. Many of the classic studies on immigrants were done in America in the 1950s and 1960s. Marks has pointed out in relation to the studies carried out before 1967, that researchers often preferred to concentrate their attention on immigrant ghettos, for the simple reason that it was more convenient to gather data from people all living in one place.[36]

Ghettos of immigrants are, however, something of a special case: often many of the customs of the country of origin are carried on within the tiny subculture of the ghetto, and where this happens residents of ghettos have their own local support structure. The demands on them are not as acute as on the immigrant who lives among natives and has to integrate. There is a hint in some studies that the children of ghetto immigrants suffer more than immigrants themselves, presumably because they have to make the biggest adaptation; from the locally upheld original traditions of their parents to those of contemporary young America.[36] In Antonovsky's terms,[23] this is the generation that lacks a sense of coherence. In those of the French sociologist Emile Durkheim, the children of immigrants are the most alienated and the most uncertain.[37] They risk falling between the two stools of the old rules and traditions of their parents and the new ones of their peers.

Michael Marmot and Leonard Syme explored this idea, that immigrant sub-communities offer protection, directly, by looking at heart disease among Japanese migrants to

California. There is a much lower rate of heart disease in Japan compared to America and when Japanese people settle in America it is well known that their rate of heart disease rises to the American rate. Yet Marmot and Syme identified a subgroup of Japanese settlers in California who had very low rates of heart disease—rates similar, in fact, to Japanese people living in Japan. Diet, it seemed, could not explain this difference. Moreover, the study was consistent with the suggestion of Marks. Those Japanese immigrants who maintained close ties with the traditional Japanese community had much lower rates of heart disease—about a fifth, in fact—than those who adopted a Western pattern of social relationships. What is more, this difference is not explained by differences in diet, serum cholesterol, smoking or blood pressure level.[38]

Japanese culture differs profoundly from that of America in many ways. The strong American ideal of individualism is not represented in Japan, where the ethic of going it alone tends to be regarded as devious. Japanese society emphasises social stability, lifelong friends and strong social ties much more than the American one does. The importance of the large Japanese companies extends far beyond the working environment. They are providers of homes, health care centres, recreational centres and shopping facilities. They also to some extent define friendships. It has been remarked that a Japanese man from the Toyota factory would seldom go out with competitors from Mitsubishi.[39] There is something almost tribe-like about this organisation which perhaps makes for a stability and order not dissimilar to that seen in primitive cultures but which we in the industrial West have all but lost.

If the difficulties of settling in a new country can be helped by a supportive social environment, so can the difficulties of moving one's home within a country. Schulz summarises the extensive literature on relocation of the elderly and its effects on health and survival thus:

Elderly people who are forced to relocate for reasons such as urban renewal, debilitating physical decline, or decreased financial resources are often stressed by the loss of a familiar and supportive environment and by the demands of coping with a new set of stimuli in an unfamiliar setting. The predominant finding is that relocation has negative effects on the elderly. Many researchers have claimed that the psychological and physical well-being of the sick and elderly are adversely affected by abrupt or severe changes in their living environment. The adverse effects are typically assessed by measures of mortality, depression and activity level.[40]

More severe changes (for example, from home to institution) have worse consequences than less severe changes (for example, from institution to institution). Whether or not the person believes he or she has a choice about moving seems to matter too. Having a choice results in better health and increased longevity.[41]

Social support seems to play an important part in crises of all kinds. Susan Gore studied 110 men who lost their jobs because of the closure of two car factories in Michigan. Those men who reported having strong support from their families and friends and an opportunity to engage in social activities suffered least in terms of poor physical and mental health.[42]

The benign influence of social support is again to be seen in pregnancy and its outcome. A study of 170 pregnant women found that complications in pregnancy, including threatened miscarriages and stillbirths, were very much more common among women experiencing stressful life events, who saw themselves as having little support from others. Complications were three times as common for those with low support as for those with high support.[43]

Conclusion

It must be restated that there are indeed difficulties in arriving at conclusions from individual pieces of research on social support of the kind reviewed in this chapter. In every case we are left wondering, is it diet, body weight, exercise, alcohol, stress, support, etc., that is responsible for the different health patterns in different groups of people? Even those studies that have made painstaking efforts to take into account and 'control for' non-psychological explanations of why one group enjoys better health than another, however powerful their statistics and subtle their analyses, do not on their own provide unambiguous proof of a causal link between stress, social support and physical health. A die-hard opponent of the hypothesis can always pick holes in any one individual report.

But the force of the research that has been done on this subject does not lie in any one outstandingly well designed and well executed study. It lies in the multi-pronged, multi-disciplinary, multi-method nature of the research —precisely in the variety of ways of approaching and investigating the subject and the richness of imagination on which these were conceived. The picture we get—a small part of which was projected in this chapter—is of many differently styled research initiatives, some a great deal more scientific than others, converging on a common finding, or theme: that an individual's physical and mental health is profoundly affected by other people. In some ways this is a surprising and challenging conclusion and in other ways it is not. It is surprising from a medical, or biochemical, standpoint because the body is traditionally regarded as a collection of organs that function or malfunction independently of anything else. Traditional medicine *has* to take this view in order to enable its repertoire of medical and surgical interventions: these are only applicable to the individual-as-organ-complex.

The message is *not* surprising in the sense that something

roughly approximating this knowledge has been in every single folk culture since knowledge began. The problem is that it has been submerged in a sea of myth, mystery and superstition. But the overwhelming consensus of modern research is clear: an individual's health depends upon the individual's standing in relation to others. The mechanism by which this works is not mysterious in any way: it is the brain-endocrine-immune system and its ramifications. The brain is the mediator in all this: stress, as it is perceived, assayed and evaluated by the individual, sets the pattern in structures of the brain that ultimately determines health or illness. And social support modulates the appraisal of stress, and on its own helps to protect health by keeping the system toned up and vigilant against natural, ever-present, pathological inclinations.

So *People Need People*, as a recent editorial in the *Lancet*[44] was entitled. The corpus of research, especially that done over the last decade, taken as a whole, has proved this beyond reasonable doubt. But exactly in what sense do people need other people? Hermits and recluses can live perfectly healthy lives. Overcrowding is notoriously bad for health. And there are moments in most people's lives when they long to be alone.

Other research has turned up good news for pet owners. Despite the risks to health that medical authorities insist are attached to living with an animal, pets, it seems, have a general therapeutic effect. One study showed that the death rate among victims of a heart attack a year after the attack was five times as great for people who did not own pets as it was for pet owners.[45] The type of pet—dog, cat, fish or lizard—did not seem to make any difference, so this finding cannot be put down to dog owners taking more exercise. Ornstein and Sobel[39] suggest that what is important here is the sense of responsibility attached to the role of pet owner, in that this provides an incentive to care for and look after an animal. But being a pet owner also creates a psychological bond with other pet owners, opening up domains of action, interaction, conversation and thought that would otherwise not exist. Pets can provide short-term benefits, too. Stroking dogs, and even the mere presence of a dog in the room, has been shown to lower blood pressure.[39]

This chapter closes with the conclusion that our health is in some way crucially dependent on other people, and that we ourselves may be instrumental in affecting the health of others. But the social nature of human beings is a complex matter and the way in which people form ties with others is a subtle affair. To arm ourselves with the means of acting on the link that is now established between health and social forces, we need to be clearer about exactly what is at stake here.

Chapter 7

STRESS AS DISCONNECTEDNESS

The work done on social support indicates it is the quality, not the quantity of support that counts in the fight against cancer.[1] But what is *quality* of support? And more fundamentally, what exactly is meant by the word 'social'?

In some ways, 'social' is a misleading term. In everyday use a person's social life means meeting people and going out with them, to parties and so forth. Psychologists and sociologists use the word in a much wider sense, and sometimes it is difficult to work out precisely what this is. Here are six definitions of social psychology chosen at random from psychology textbooks:

1 'Social psychology is the scientific study of human interaction.'

2 'Social psychology is a subdiscipline of psychology that especially involves the scientific study of the behaviour of individuals as a function of social stimuli.'

3 'Social psychology is the study of the way in which individuals are affected by social situations.'

4 'Social psychology is the scientific study of personal and situational factors that affect individual social behaviour.'

5 'Social psychology: A discipline that attempts to understand, explain, and predict how the thoughts, feelings and actions of individuals are influenced by the perceived, imagined, or implied thoughts, feelings and actions of others.'

6 'Social psychology is a scientific attempt to understand and explain how the thoughts, feelings, and behaviour of individuals are influenced by the actual, imagined, or implied presence of others.'

There are problems with 2, 3 and 4. They all beg the question of what is meant by 'social' by involving the word tautologically, as part of the definition. 1, 2, 3 and 4 all seem to want to tie us down to direct face-to-face meetings between people. Only 5 and 6 acknowledge the influence of others in their absence, through their mental presence in a person's thoughts, feelings and imaginings. Our experience tells us this must be right and that the imprint of others is carried far beyond actual meetings with them. One of the most profound ways one person can have an effect on another is through his or her death and permanent absence.

We saw in the previous chapter that many of those writing about social support and illness believe it is lack of *participation* rather than lack of support *per se* that is responsible for the higher rates of illness and death seen in the unsupported groups of people studied. By 'participation' is meant having an established place in the social network—being actively involved through having a role or set of roles—for example: 'Among the elderly in Finnish society, extensive social participation reflects an active involvement in society and embeddedness in a social system, a way-of-life which is characterized by social competence and active social interaction in general. Thus it may rather be one's way-of-life as a totality than the pattern of social participation as such which is protective. This view is consistent with the suggestion that social support could be seen as one component of a more general concept, control of one's destiny.'[2] Professor Leaf's conclusions about the healthy elderly populations in isolated rural settlements (see Chapter 6) fit closely with these remarks.

Every society and social organisation is bound by some

system of rules, roles and mutual expectancies—this is what defines it. This applies even in the smallest possible social unit, that made up of just two people—a couple who decide to get married or live together, for example. In deciding this, there is a presumption of mutual expectancy and reciprocity of some kind.

The essence of being *social*, the way the word is used by more enlightened social scientists, is really a very simple matter. It comes down to *sharing*. And yet the way humans share is not that simple. It is simple enough in social species other than humans. Social animals co-operate and share in a stereotyped way that is the direct product of genetics and instinct. Their social nature gives them a biological advantage over non-social species since things like nest-building, bringing up young and getting food can be accomplished jointly, which is more efficient and allows predators to be kept at bay at the same time.

Humans are a quantum leap more complicated: we are unique in our ability to devise and manipulate symbols. By far the most important system of symbols we use is language. A primate starts grieving over the loss of its partner only when the loss becomes physically apparent—the partner is seen to have died, or is physically missed. A person starts grieving after a tragic telephone message. A very great deal of our social life—in the sense of sharing—is played out in words and talk. Most of the scientific studies of social support that have been done, and all of the large-scale ones, did not place enough weight on this very important instrument of social support. This is bound to have had the effect of underestimating the importance of social support in health. Only the detailed studies, like those of the sociologist George Brown, took into account the detailed nature of social relationships and thus were able to reveal the extent of the importance of having a confidant—someone close to talk to.

THE PRACTICAL AND THE EXPRESSIVE

In societies that are materially replete, that is, where there is an abundance of resources and an economic surplus, most of us no longer have to worry about basic needs. We have enough food, perhaps too much, we have adequate shelter and we can keep warm in the cold winters and cool in the hot summers. Even in pre-industrial societies, anthropologists calculate that only eight to ten per cent of living time is given over to sustenance of life. That leaves a lot of time for other activities.

The philosopher Rom Harré has pointed out that having one's basic needs met, and more, brings about a fundamental shift in the way social life is lived.[3] True, we have to work to earn a living, but in the working environment as well as outside it, a great deal of our time is devoted to proving and parading our social worth. We do this in numerous ways by exhibiting our familiarity with the rules of the games that make up social interaction. We like to test and show off our competence and capabilities to other people. Societies offer an enormous range of opportunities for this, from formal honours, positions and investitures, to the clothes we wear, the cars we drive, the holidays we take and the jokes we tell. But the richest domain of expressive activity is our ordinary everyday conversation, where attitudes and opinions are aired, others come in for praise or ridicule, and our sense of self is thereby reinforced and sharpened.

Men and women who have faced the tough task of establishing themselves in new surroundings—immigrants and settlers, for example—may well throw up their hands in horror at this picture of man with so much time for indulging the expressive side of life. There have indeed been periods in human history when practical efforts so engulfed mankind as to be the overwhelming influence on social formations. An outstanding example is the industrial revolution in nineteenth-century Europe. Marx and

Engels, in *The German Ideology*, elaborate their influential theory of social structure and power from an analysis of the forces controlling the means of production, 'The first historical act is thus the production of the means to satisfy these (practical) needs, the production of material life itself . . .'

In nineteenth-century Europe maybe; but perhaps this period in man's history was something of an aberration. Harré sums up this criticism, tongue-in-cheek, thus, 'Marx said that it was in the nature of man to work. Not at least as the human race is presently constituted. It is in the nature of men to slip off to the pub to display their *machismo*, and of women to exchange anecdotes about the prowess of their children.'[3]

The distinction between the practical and expressive arenas of social life is of passing interest rather than central importance to the main concern of this book: the conditions of health and illness. The nature of the social order in which one chooses to move, or is compelled to move, is not important. What *is* important for health is that the individual has a sense of 'belonging', through actively participating in a moral order of *some* kind—be it practical or expressive. A moral order contains rules and standards that enable and regulate actions and that are by definition shared with other people. In the practical domain, rules and standards revolve around physical competence, the accomplishment of work and survival. In the expressive domain, they are concerned with social worth.

THE SOCIAL AND THE SOLITARY

A person can be totally alone yet engaged in an activity that is social. Take gardening as an example. This is something that does not require the presence of others; yet it is fundamentally a social activity because a gardener is a follower of rules and the activities of gardening are directed towards ends and goals that are already laid down. Its desiderata and aesthetics have previously been defined by a community and are therefore socially 'given'. The way a well-kept garden should look comes from a consensus: it should not be full of weeds and dead plants; it should give the impression of order and control . . . etc. These are qualities that can be recognised and appreciated by other members of the gardening fraternity. Differences of opinion there may be, just as there are in any area of human endeavour, but a core of shared attitudes underpins the nature of the activity and its worth. Of course it does not have to be a solitary business: going to flower shows, meeting at clubs, the mutual admiration of friends, all provide good opportunities for meetings with other people.

The point is, however, that a person *can* spend many hours on their own, gardening or studying or practising a musical instrument or writing a book, and in doing so they are doing something social because they are following (or breaking) rules, and rules are the property and expression of institutions. Such 'institutions' need not be as dry and constraining as the term implies. The four examples I have given all contain scope for originality and invention. Creativity is something that is much debated and admired, but following the rules or breaking the rules both depend upon a high intimacy with them. As scholars of the history of art like to show, innovations rely on a flow of forms whose continuity can be demonstrated. In breaking, and hence extending, the rules and creating new forms from old ones, an individual exhibits a close familiarity and connection with the social formations they represent.

There are some good examples of activities that were done in private, yet were essentially social in intent, in the things that helped prisoners survive the harsh conditions of the Nazi concentration camps: great value was placed on these activities as a psychological aid to survival. Very few actual co-operative partnerships, relationships or groups of friends grew up and flourished among prisoners, partly because the regime did not tolerate them and partly because socialising takes energy and there was insufficient of this even to look after one's basic biological needs. However, many of the survivors writing about their experiences describe the moment of their decision to embark on a project which, isolated though they were in its carrying out, had the liberating effect of reinstating them as members of the normal, sane, moral world (see the accounts in Chapter 4).[4]

The moment of such decisions marks a psychological liberation rather than a physical one, but the effect goes deep. Many ex-prisoners have written of the illuminating effect of their decision to keep an illegal diary of the goings-on at the camps where they were interned, so that those in the free world should come to know about them and prevent the same thing ever happening again. Other prisoners determined to preserve some sense of personal dignity by using all their energy and guile to obtain soap, shaving gear and clothes so as to stay clean—a very difficult task. Others kept up some sort of private observance of religious ritual and prayer.

These are all moral projects taken on by individuals in an environment run on the immoral canons of hatred and cruelty. They belong to a different world—the world of sanity, dignity and tolerance. As such, these lonely projects were able to provide prisoners with an umbilical cord linking them with that world, even though the prisoners themselves were physically far removed from it. They managed to cheat the system by achieving a psychological liberty through a commitment to something that was part of a valued world, and through an active psychological participation and a sharing in that world. Reports of survivors are not scientific evidence, but fighting back and survival are consistently linked, in the writings of these people, to the taking on of such a project. It restored the sense of being a person.

CHOICE AND FEELINGS OF CONTROL OVER ONE'S DESTINY

How much choice a person has, or feels he has, in what he is doing is known to be important in determining his feelings of fulfilment and personal satisfaction. The affluent free world is varied and pluralistic; the spectrum of alternatives from which to choose, in one's work as well as outside it, can be very wide indeed. A prisoner assigned to look after the commandant's garden is in a very different psychological position from someone who chooses gardening as a work or recreational activity of his own free will. Intuitively, something you do because you have chosen to do it carries a lot more psychological weight than something you are forced into.

In the 1970s we carried out a small experiment on the subject of choice, using volunteers who were inpatients at University College Hospital, London.[5] The patients were people who were not seriously ill. They were suffering from some form of chest complaint and were mainly at the hospital for observation and tests. None of them was able to sleep properly at night in spite of being given sleeping pills. What we did was to stop the ineffective medication and give all the patients placebos—pills with no organic effect at all—the classic 'sugar pill'. There were blue ones and green ones; both were chemically identical and inactive. The patients believed they were being asked to participate in a trial evaluating two new drugs and were given a phoney story about each. They were told that both were new sleeping pills and that each had different properties and it was thought the green one would suit some people best and the blue one, others . . . etc.

What colour pill a person received was in fact irrelevant: the purpose was to study the effect of having a choice. Half the patients were given a choice as to which pill they would like to try and the other half were not—they were just told they would be getting either the blue one or the green one.

All the patients were monitored through the night by the nursing staff. Those given a choice slept much better, as a consequence of the dummy treatment, than those not given a choice, because they felt they had more of a psychological investment in it. To our embarrassment, three patients who were given the choice insisted on prescriptions for the 'drug' after they had left the ward!

It seems likely that the placebo effect forms part of every medical and therapeutic manoeuvre. It also seems surgery is no exception. In the mid-1950s a new surgical procedure was introduced for the relief of chest pain. This was called 'internal mammary ligation' and involved tying off an artery in the chest. Almost all the patients treated with this procedure reported an improvement in their symptoms. Many reported considerable improvement and these reports were backed up by electrocardiogram printouts.

As always happens when success is claimed for a new medical treatment, this gives rise to a lot of publicity and a queue of people wanting it. A few surgeons nevertheless remained sceptical about the procedure, and an interesting test was run on its medical efficacy. An experiment was carried out in which candidates for the operation were randomly assigned to receive either the artery-tying operation itself or a placebo operation in which the chest was cut open and sewn up again without anything else being done. The placebo surgery was found to be every bit as effective as the artery-tying operation, and the latter was eventually abandoned. But only after much hype, and an estimated 10,000 to 15,000 operations had been carried out with an average mortality from the operation of five per cent.[6]

The placebo effect is well known in medicine. It has led more than one doctor to comment rather cynically that as many patients as possible should be treated with a new procedure before its novelty and the enthusiasm for it wear off.[7]

Today it would not be possible to carry out a test such as the one just described, of a surgical treatment versus a placebo. It would be considered unethical by the committees who license medical research. But there are hints that a placebo effect may be at work in modern procedures, for instance, coronary artery bypass surgery. In this operation veins are taken from the patient's leg and used to bypass diseased arteries supplying the heart. Again the initial response to the operation was enthusiastic. Almost everyone treated reported improvement in symptoms and did better on exercise tests. There was the usual exaggerated reporting in the popular press about the new 'miracle operation', but when heart function was tested objectively, using the cold science of medical instrumentation, of those who claimed they felt better, only about 20 per cent showed real improvement, another 60 per cent showed no change, and 20 per cent were worse off.[8]

Major surgery is an alarming prospect. It is often recommended by a doctor but it cannot be forced on a person. There is always a choice, and this is made explicit by asking the patient to sign a form of consent. The direct physical benefits from many forms of surgery have been proven beyond doubt; but mixed up with these, as with all medical treatments, are undoubtedly placebo effects. This sometimes makes the relative contributions of medical and psychological factors to the patient's improvement difficult to gauge.

Medicine existed as a profession long before science. Throughout the centuries doctors and quacks have peddled a bizarre array of curative substances and procedures; the catalogue of these, even in medieval Europe, is extremely long. Virtually none of them have since been found to offer any organic benefit at all.[9] The procedures themselves were pretty arbitrary and if they worked, they almost certainly did so through the mechanism of the placebo effect.

Although there were thousands of these treatments, it is possible to state a simple formula that governs them all: take anything that is either nasty, expensive or difficult to obtain, wrap it up in mystery, and you have a cure.

Leeches, hot irons on the skin, needles, urine and faeces, are just a few examples of the enormous repertoire of extremely unpleasant treatments that were on offer at some stage throughout history. The royal touch, the touch of a hanged man, and a pilgrimage to a healing shrine are examples of cures that involved considerable effort and difficulty on the part of the patient. In 1925 Janet made the interesting observation that a long and arduous pilgrimage to the shrine at Lourdes increased the chance of a 'cure': cures were rare for the local inhabitants.[10] Throughout centuries medicinal gold and gold solutions remained fashionable among those able to afford them. One eighteenth-century British doctor was prosecuted by the Royal College of Physicians for charging £6 for a single pill.

The psychology behind all this again comes down to the matter of personal choice and commitment on the part of the individual. It is no use prescribing neutral and inexpensive things as treatments, as these are just too available; the patient would not have to *do* anything to get them. Remedies have to be nasty, difficult or expensive so as to require the psychological investment that comes with making any definite decision.

The choice to receive major surgery is one that most of us would rather not have to make. The numerous choices between over-the-counter brand names available in chemist's shops is, on the other hand, a more lightweight matter. There are so many of these one may as well choose at random. Could this be why more people are turning to alternative treatments, like homeopathy? Does the act of choosing one of these (and thereby rejecting traditional medicine) in itself carry more psychological investment and therefore more meaning?

Attributions

The issue of personal choice and control is central to our understanding of the psychology of health. Yet it is not entirely straightforward. Two people can be in the same job, and one sees it as rewarding and enjoyable and full of opportunities and scope for personal choice, while the other sees it as a dead end with no promise and no way out. What is important here is not so much freedom to choose in any absolute sense but a person's *perception* of how much choice he or she has. A 'feeling of control over one's destiny' is something that is often mentioned as a guardian of health, in the literature concerned with stress and illness.

Some people, no matter how many choices and opportunities others might see as spread out in front of them, believe their lives are shaped and controlled by outside forces, or 'destiny'. Psychologists have a measure for this facet of personality known as *Locus of Control*.[11] At the one extreme there are people who reckon that, no matter what befalls them, they have some measure of control—they tend always to feel instrumental in what they do and responsible for their decisions and actions. At the other are those who believe there is little they can do to affect anything—their life is shaped by immutable forces. The survivors of the death camps, who created for themselves a microcosm of choice and commitment in an environment where total repression and control reigned supreme, are an outstanding example of the first category of person. Perhaps the strange malaise of multi-millionaires, like Howard Hughes, who ended up as a depressed recluse, shutting himself away from the world in a hotel penthouse, is an example of the second. In any case, people who see themselves as having choices and being able to act effectively on the world they live in, enjoy generally better physical and mental health than those who feel controlled and put upon.[12]

The fact that having choices and feeling free is more than anything a state of mind is recognised by psychologists and forms part of an important set of ideas known as *Attribution Theory*.[13] Choice is something that people *attribute* to themselves and their lives. The power of Attribution Theory as a therapeutic tool lies in the belief that one's mental attitudes

—one's *attributions*—about various things, including how much control one has, can be changed.[14] Campaigns through the media to stop young people smoking are based on the same idea: 'You don't have to smoke just because your friends do. YOU can resist peer pressure' . . . 'Even if your parents smoke, you don't have to imitate them. YOU can decide for yourself' . . . 'Cigarette ads are a rip-off! YOU can resist media pressure to smoke.'

A similar technique is used to treat clinical depression.[15] Depression is characterised by sadness, apathy and withdrawal. The therapist tries to get the patient to initiate actions, at first in a small way, and then builds up from this an attitude of personal control over outcomes which, if the therapy is successful, the patient generalises to other aspects of her life. The underlining of an individual's choice is an old trick among therapists: 'You've already taken the most important step by deciding to get treatment' . . . 'The real initiative has got to come from you' . . . etc. The theory is that gradually, a person's belief that she controls her own destiny is restored, and the vicious circle of apathy, depression and illness can be turned round into the virtuous one of activity, happiness and health (Fig. 17).

Sometimes people become clinically depressed for the opposite reason—they develop deep-seated feelings of low self-esteem through wrongly attributing misfortunes to themselves . . . 'I must be inferior because people don't smile at me when I walk down the street,' or, 'Why have I got this illness? It must be a punishment.' In such cases therapy is aimed at getting the person to attribute the cause of the misfortune to environmental, or 'external' forces rather than to herself.

The technique of getting people to attribute misfortunes to outside sources rather than to themselves was used to help solve a problem that American military psychiatrists had to deal with during the war in Vietnam. Men in established combat units, with experience of battle and the conditions of life away from home in Vietnam, were in the

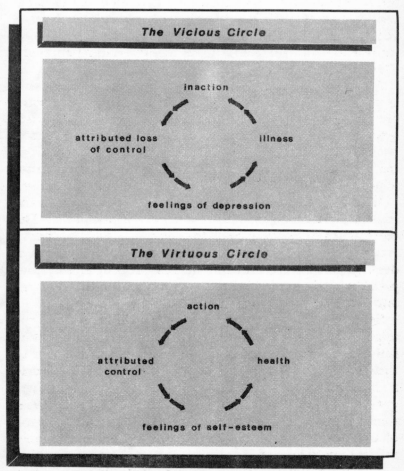

Fig. 17   The vicious and virtuous circles.

habit of greeting new arrivals with hostility and suspicion. The newcomer, unfamiliar with everything, especially the unwritten rules of the unit, was clumsy and naïve to his seasoned companions. Novices became known as 'f.n.gs' —fucking new guys: the result was a considerable number of psychiatric casualties among the new men. Psychiatrists were to some extent able to prevent this happening by explaining the generality of the situation to a newcomer, and getting him to understand that 'they hate the fucking new guy' does not mean 'they hate me'. In this way the hostility could be attributed by those on the receiving end to an outside, situational cause—a category—rather than to a personal one.

Attribution therapists use various techniques to replace attitudes of helplessness and negativity with attitudes of effectiveness—in particular the attitude that one has control over one's life. This is referred to by various names, 'personal control training', 'assertiveness training', 'social skills training', 'cognitive restructuring', and so forth. The essence of these therapies is that someone (the therapist) injects meaning into someone else's (the client's) life using professional techniques to change attitudes about the self. Such techniques are not totally removed from those of brain-washing; but attribution therapy differs from brain-washing in one important respect: its objective is not a political one, it is simply the removal of disabling symptoms and the restoration of health in the individual. Whatever the form therapy takes, and there are many schools of thought about this, it is accomplished through two people meeting and exchanging words.

A version of the same thing is of course going on all the time in everyday life. Our friends may lack the formal training of the attribution therapist, but their help and encouragement runs along recognisably similar lines: 'OK, so you didn't get the job. Maybe the job didn't suit you. You'll just have to stop whining and find a better one' . . . 'Every cloud has a silver lining' . . . etc. Episodes like this are a familiar part of life. They are like attribution therapy in that they are attempts to get a person to take on a more positive attitude about his effectiveness and powers, and they too rely on an interchange between two people.

I emphasise this last point because the theme of this chapter, and indeed of this book, is that an individual's psychological well-being and physical health are dependent in a fundamental way on other people. This applies both to the maintenance of health, which works through our involvement with others keeping the brain-immune system fine-tuned and effective, and to the restoration of health in cases where attributions of helplessness and hopelessness result in depression and physical dysfunction. Social support supports the psyche and the body (both part of the same unity) by a process of psychological preventive inoculation in well people, and through psychological intervention in sick ones. But as in physical medicine, intervention is often too late and the best results are achieved through prevention.

LANGUAGE

That language occupies a central position in our social lives needs no proving. Our appetite for gossip and conversation is insatiable and there are many roles of language besides that of a straight carrier of information. 'Your dinner's on the table', can be a neutral statement of fact or, depending on the context and the tone in which it is said, it can be a criticism, a rebuff, a challenge or even a statement of love. A great deal of people's time is taken up with expressive talk—conversations about likes, dislikes, criticisms and praise of others, and the performance and self-display that is part of telling jokes and stories.

Whatever the talk is about, language provides us with a medium for sharing, be it information, views, judgements, shock or laughter. The philosopher and linguist, John Searle, sees language as so bound up with action as to be part of the same process.[16] Actions and language are both rule-governed forms of behaviour and both are ultimately answerable to the institutions of social life. The notion that social order is inherent in the conversations we have with one another is more or less assumed by the philosophers in the French structuralist tradition.[17]

The same basic idea lies behind the modern study, *sociolinguistics*: 'Language as speaking practice creates and identifies social group membership. Through shared communicative conventions, individuals treat each other as part of their own social group. It is this that enables them to acquire knowledge and experience which reinforce the social group and sharedness.'[18]

A very neat exposition of this point was made by the troubled Austrian philosopher, Ludwig Wittgenstein. Wittgenstein[19,20] exposed the essentially social, or shared, nature of language by attacking the idea of a 'private' language—the idea that it is possible for a commentary to take place that is comprehensible only to the speaker and no one else. Could one imagine talking to someone, even in one's thoughts, without there being an audience, an object of the talk—someone to hear and understand what was being said or thought? From the impossibility of private languages he deduced that all talk must be based on rules and, logically, rules are the property of social networks: of institutions. He coined the term 'language games' to refer to conversational exchanges between people. He went on to reason that there must be a logical link between the individual's social world and his or her speech and mental life. He regarded language, along with all other forms of rule-based activity, such as mathematics, gardening, playing chess or doing scientific experiments, as an anthropological phenomenon. Words, sentences, symbols and squiggles come to have meaning and value on account of their shared nature and the consensus of the social institutions that govern their use. Institutions are there in the background even in the most insignificant exchanges between people. Even comments passed about the weather are to be seen as social acts.

Again, 'institution' is too stiff a word to describe some social units—a pair of lovers, for instance. But two is enough for a social unit and one sees perhaps the nearest thing there is to a private language in the special words and catchphrases couples often start to use to one another and to nobody else when they become close. Such words and phrases are expressions of the intimate and exclusive character of the relationship.

Wittgenstein refuses to divorce the study of language from the study of those who speak it. His theory of language is built on the insight that the meaning of utterances arises out of their practice in a community—'If we had to name anything which is the life of the sign we should have to say that it was its *use*.'[20] Wittgenstein died in 1951 and so would not have been aware of the recent discoveries linking an individual's involvement with the social world, the workings of the brain and immune system, and health and survival. If he had, then he would have appreciated that 'life' in this passage really does mean Life.

So what is stress? Summary

We are now in a position to draw together the evidence presented and the arguments aired in this book into some kind of a theory of that slippery concept, psychological stress. I have tried to show that despite the rough and provisional definitions of stress that have been used as a basis for research, despite the different and to some extent competing schools of thought on the subject, and despite the difficulties in doing and interpreting research, the case is now proved that psychological stress profoundly affects a person's physical health. Moreover, it does so in a much more potent and subtle way than do variations in the diet which, within limits, are compensated for by the body's own internal chemistry. So what is stress?

Stress in modern man is fundamentally a social, not a physical matter. In the end, social forms are stronger than physical ones and in social species, including humans, the collective is ascendant over the individual. Why else are people prepared to die for causes?

In humans, social life is complex and subtle. Physical meetings between people make up an important part of it, but not the only part and probably not the main part. The 'social' can find expression in all sorts of symbolic ways, especially through language. Talk of 'underlying social structures', 'social networks', etc., seems rather vague and abstract, but any theory of stress that concerns itself with symbolic forms, and hence meaning, must be permitted a degree of abstraction. Abstraction but not obscurism. The circumstances under which stress occurs can be summarised under two headings.

1   Traumatic life changes

A sudden traumatic event, such as the death of someone close, or imprisonment in a concentration camp, involves loss. What is lost is any opportunity to choose and act in a meaningful way. This is the same as saying the person becomes cut off from sources of sharing and participating with others by being part of a social, or moral, order.

The 'loss' suffered in this variety of circumstances has to be seen as symbolic—a loss of meaning—an abstract isolation—an aloneness that is relevant beyond physical proximity and company. What is stressed beyond its elastic limit, and breaks, is the umbilical cord between the individual and the collective. This is a psychological matter.

2   Coping and personality

Some people deal with life's traumas better than others. They appear to be better equipped to cope. They have the ability and the sense to make a realistic assessment of the situation and the energy to adapt by taking on new goals and fresh commitments.

Suzanne Kobasa, a social psychologist with a special interest in personalities that are able to resist stress, made a study of executives in a large American company during a period when that company was preparing for major re-organisation and rationalisation.[21] It was a time of considerable stress and uncertainty among the employees. Her findings in a way summarise much of the work on the resilient person. Those people who suffered least from the changes, in terms of both mental and physical well-being, are described as having a strong sense of *commitment*—to their work, their families, their friends and themselves, and a strong sense of overall control over their lives which gave them a certain flexibility and tolerance of change.

The fighting spirit of those prisoners who stood against camp life provides an extraordinary example of resilience through commitment. Again, the fight is a psychological one rather than a physical one. It involves freely chosen (or freely attributed) action and the salvaging for oneself of a moral career. In this way the break in the umbilical cord between individual and social is repaired and the threat to health averted.

Unfortunately there do appear to be extremes of personality that are particularly disadvantageous in times of stress and change. These are characteristics which hinder and block coping on account of their grip on a person's life. Even worse, research seems to be telling us that for some personalities, the situation is bleak in that the way a person is can by itself be maladaptive, even when life is going smoothly. Two traits in particular predispose to illness: the Type-A person and the denying suppressing, 'everything's all right' person (see the discussion in Chapter 3).

The Type-A's rigidly hostile, single-minded, Sisyphus-like striving is not the best way of connecting with other people. The denier's pervading over-concern with niceness and social acceptability represents another form of rigidity also bound to create difficulties on account of a flawed and unrealistic perception of events, especially internal biological impulses such as anger, whose expression gets blocked.

The Type-A and the suppressor-denier are similar. They both exhibit an almost obsessional need to prove themselves; to appear worthy in the eyes of others. And in the extremity of their styles—in their very obsessiveness—is the whiff of failure. They are both examples of desperate and unsatisfied strivings for social recognition: the Type-A through his bull-dozing efforts to complete an overloaded schedule—which is never completed—and the suppressor-denier through his strict adherence to an imagined, inflexible 'ideal' social code which is given ascendance over reality. The hall-mark of both these styles is their inability to achieve, or feel they achieve, or attribute to themselves, their goal. Neither succeeds in the realisation of a social self. Their single-minded, self-perpetuating nature, like the free-spinning cog that fails to mesh and engage with its parent counterpart, betrays an underlying social malaise.

Nevertheless, it is important to remember that these personalities are extremes and that the majority of us are able to strike a good balance. Much speculation and research has gone into the background of these traits and not surprisingly the way a child is brought up is strongly implicated as the main cause in both cases: the overambitious parent in the case of Type-As and the strict and up-tight moralist in the case of the suppressor-denier. On the brighter side, research indicates that both these extreme characteristics can be modified through therapy. We shall return to this in the final chapter.

CONCLUSION

Stressful life events, coping and personality are related concepts. The research and the ideas discussed under each heading overlap and interrelate. The thesis of this book is that all stressful (that is, life-threatening) psychological conditions have the same common denominator—the powerlessness of the person to engage in activities of a social origin, and his or her consequent isolation from any of the pockets of social order that make up our complex, pluralistic societies. A person needs to share and participate in *some* way for life to be meaningful and for the chemistry of the healthy body to remain intact.

We have noted that social organisation is not unique to humans. Numerous species—insects, birds, fish and mammals—exhibit it, and it is fascinating to see the forms that it can take. Biologists are keen to point out the advantages in terms of survival that social organisation brings. Level of evolutionary development is often measured by the degree of division of labour and co-operation within a species. Insects are believed to be among the first to have colonised land about 400 million years ago. They have had plenty of time to evolve communities in which there is specialisation, especially with regard to the distribution of food and the defence of territory. Ants are one of the most social of insects in this respect: almost all their activities are run on a social basis. Many species of ant farm aphids and construct pens where the aphids are fed and milked for the nutritious honey they secrete.

Arrangements between individuals involving co-operation and mutual obligation are common, too, in monkeys and chimpanzees. Long-lasting cliques and partnerships have been described among the females in troops of rhesus monkeys and among male baboons. A male baboon will enlist the help of a friend in gaining access to a female, and may later be called upon to return the favour. Biologists call this *reciprocal altruism*. The friendships and loyalties that grow up are not necessarily restricted to kin.[22]

The great advantage, in terms of survival, that social species have over species that are not social is that the pooled resources of an organised social unit are far greater than the sum of the individual resources of those that make up the unit. A well trained army is much more effective than a rabble.

Social organisation in many species, including man, has evolved as a powerful aid to the perpetuation of that species. In animals other than man the physical forms which the expression of this organisation takes are highly stereotyped. The commentator on *The Natural World* says with confidence, 'This display of plumage is the first stage in the mating process.' Social behaviour all happens under a rigid genetic programme. In man, as we have noted, the ability to communicate through symbols puts the whole business on a different footing: a very great deal of our social interaction is not directly related to survival and reproduction, and its forms are not stereotyped and predictable.

The period of development from baby to mature adult is extraordinarily long in human beings. Unlike any other primate, the human brain develops *outside* the womb. Vital to the process of its development is its exposure to the outside world—to the world of things, of symbols and, especially, of other people. The brain, in close communication with the immune system, grows and develops not in isolation but by making links with other brains and at the same time exerting a reciprocal influence on their development.

It is therefore not enough to say that a developing child's brain 'receives' information and instruction during the course of its long development—passively, like a repository. It matures through interaction with others. Its formations are not exactly the *result* of the information culled from meeting and talking with others, they are at one and the same time an embodiment and an expression of it. Such is the depth of man's social nature that there is no point in drawing too fine a line between the 'social', the symbols and signs in which social forms are expressed, and the workings of the human brain itself. Any severance of the link between the individual animal and the social person constitutes a threat to the whole business—psyche and brain and, if you like, soul. In particular, the brain's control over itself, over the rest of the nervous system, over hormones and over the immune system, is undermined. The unity of the complex system on which health depends fails to hold up, and health comes under siege. Evolution has assigned so crucial and extended a role to man's social nature that the animal—old biological man—can no longer exist without it.[23]

Chapter 8

COPING AND STAYING HEALTHY

The *internal* theory of health has a great many things to say about how to look after one's health and how to help others look after theirs. Prescriptions for good health are rather more subtle than those the pharmacist prepares, or those the dietician recommends. Treatment with drugs and diet regards the person as a biological black box. Treatments explored in this chapter regard him or her as both an individual and a social being—the two inextricably bound up with one another. They demand an outlook less simplistic than choosing from a list of foods, or pharmacopœia of drugs.

We saw in Chapter 6 that providing people with social support—whether this is by holding the hand of an expectant mother, introducing art and music activities into a deprived ghetto or encouraging a sense of control and responsibility in an old persons' home—results in healthy changes in mood and physiology, and reduces illnesses and deaths. So the message with respect to social support must be seek it and do not withhold it. No great leap of imagination is needed to tailor the right action to a particular person in a particular situation. The crucial role of language, however, must be emphasised. Much of the research done indicates that having a friend who is also a confidant is a particularly effective weapon against the potentially harmful effects of stress. The importance of language in the giving and receiving of social support cannot be overstated.

Letting people talk
Merely listening to what people have to say is providing

them with social support. Social workers are well aware of this and put it into practice in their professional dealings with others. The elderly, the sick and the handicapped are restricted in their opportunities for expression through action. If mobility is poor and physical energy low, very often the only kinds of acts and actions available are illocutionary ones—'speech acts', to use John Searle's phrase—or, less academically, ordinary talk. Actually Searle's phrase is a good one because it underlines the point that talking is a kind of acting—a performance which helps reaffirm the self and self-esteem. Social work with old people places considerable value on encouraging them to reminisce about the past.[1] The presence of a listening ear by itself helps justify the life of the speaker and vindicate his or her social worth. To reminisce about actions taken and opinions expressed in the past is to revive moral personae that have been lived out and rehearse the all-important sense of personal control and effectiveness from which such personae sprang.

Therapy involving groups

Therapy groups, encounter groups and training groups (perhaps better known as T-groups) are enjoying increased popularity. The differently named groups have different emphases but they are all essentially the same in their objective: all of them consist in a small number of individuals allowing themselves to be closeted away with no distractions for a fixed period of time—sometimes hours, sometimes whole weekends. Talking freely and openly in the group is actively, even aggressively, encouraged. J. Kovel captures the flavour of group therapy in this passage:

> When one is enmeshed in group life, the outside world fades away, the constraints of reality vanish, and less adulterated forms of our inner selves clamber onto the stage. Loyalties reminiscent of groups in war, whose

members would unhesitatingly die for one another; raptures comparable to those of the monastery; jealousies forgotten since age four; power plays worthy of a Borgia; tender intimacy one could never muster with one's spouse—it can all be summoned up within the group.[2]

Members of these groups often disagree and shout at one another, but they hold a psychological membership card, from the start, owing to their initial commitment of wanting to be part of the group. Everyone starts out with a contract to play the same 'language games', to use Wittgenstein's term. As the session wears on a common rhetorical ground develops and the group starts to behave rather like a single social organism. Individuals who have participated in these groups often speak of the strong forces that develop in them and of a sense of personal loss when the session is finished.

Here is a concentrated, microcosmic version of the social world at large. Whether people in therapy groups agree or disagree, shout at one another or even have fights (which is not unknown), the group provides a tremendously strong source of social support. Choosing to come together, stay for the duration and disclose all kinds of personal information is choosing to share a great deal.

Occupational therapy
The known rehabilitative effects of occupational therapy, although this is not always done in groups, and although it does not generate the same emotional electricity as encounters in groups, also works by helping to establish, or re-establish, the psychological link between the individual and the collective. Even if you are doing things on your own, you are actively participating and sharing because the goals you are working towards are never random goals: they belong to a collective. The product is social in essence since its origins lie in consensus. People vary greatly in

whether they like to work alone or with others. However, doing things—striving towards chosen goals—helps the person maintain the psychological condition necessary for a sense of self and the physiological one necessary for health.

The greater the choice involved in action, the greater the psychological investment of the person. Attribution Theory tells us the important thing is not choice in any absolute sense, but *attributed* choice—how much choice a person thinks they have in doing something. The placebo pill given to hospital patients as a sleeping drug (Chapter 7) worked much better when the patients were led to believe they had a choice. The trick of getting someone to do something and then encouraging them to think their action was self-initiated is an old one. It is used in many different forms of therapy.

As a general rule, jobs that involve scope for decision and imagination are preferred to routine repetitive jobs and result in better psychological functioning and better health.[3,4] But in this, as in everything else, people vary so much that it would be absurd to pronounce on how much complexity and decision latitude is ideal in a job. What represents challenge and interest to one person may be an intolerable burden to another. Conversely, a routine task, such as cataloguing, may be very satisfying or crushingly boring, depending upon who you are. Attribution Theory puts the whole business on a subjective footing through its premise that the most important thing, psychologically, is *attributed* choice—that is, how much scope for action and decision a person reads into what he or she is doing.

From the therapeutic perspective this shift in emphasis is extremely important. It allows the therapist to think in terms of manipulating and changing a person's attributions to therapeutic advantage, without in any way compromising the validity of what the person believes to be true. This is primarily a theoretical move: by centring the theory on what a person thinks about a situation, or what attributions he makes about it, the therapist is in effect saying, 'Let's for the sake of therapy treat all the potential attributions a person makes as equally valid. Because then we can set about juggling with them and no one is entitled to use the word "deception"'.[5] Such a stand confers on a therapist considerable power and is clearly not without its political caveats.

*   *   *

These remarks about social support and its application in everyday life, while they are general remarks, are of fundamental importance with respect to how we can apply our knowledge and understanding of stress and coping to the world. The ideas aired in this book give us not so much a set of standard procedures for coping with stress as a generative formula which has considerable relevance to what people can do to help themselves and others stay well, with an indefinite number of applications.

The general idea of social support as a source of health is summarised in Fig. 18. This shows three concentric circles: the inner circle marks the domain of shared commitment, effective action, psychological well-being and health; the outer circle represents total isolation and the inability to maintain a sense of self and to survive.

Such isolation, it is important to remember, is a symbolic, psychological matter rather than a physical aloneness: it is the failure of the individual to connect with any of the social formations that thread through our species, in terms of which life comes to holds meaning. It is the breakdown of action, choice and agency. In between are various levels of connectedness, the middle circle representing the risk to health that threatens when a person's resources are challenged in times of stress. Social support is drawn as a force driving towards the centre. Being aware of the psychological conditions of health and the powerful role of social support is itself the strongest piece of armour a person can have in the war against stress.

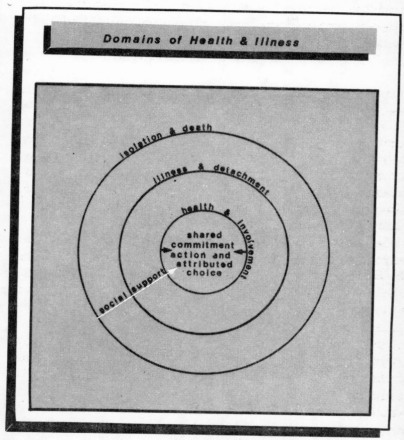

Fig. 18   Sharing goals and ideals with others helps protect
health.

SPECIFIC REMEDIES AND TREATMENTS

So much for generalisations. What about more specific action? We have identified (Chapter 3) two personality traits that seem particularly harmful to health—the Type-A pattern and a characteristic suppression and denial of all things unpleasant, especially negative emotions like hate and anger. The origins of these unfortunate traits probably lie in upbringing. Nevertheless, is it possible to do anything about them?

Any personality characteristic is somewhat resistant to change, otherwise it would not endure and persist over time so as to be a recognisable characteristic. Several attempts have been made to modify the obsessional Type-A trait. The conclusion reached, in a recent review of the 18 studies that have been done, is positive: 'We conclude that psychologic intervention to reduce Type-A behaviour pattern may improve clinical outcome of coronary heart disease and that this deserves further study and preliminary clinical application.'[6]

This research on modifying maladaptive personality patterns is still young and there is as yet no agreed standard way of 'treating' Type-A. A variety of techniques has been tried: simple educational programmes informing people of the relation between Type-A and heart disease, courses of relaxation training, yoga, attribution therapy (for example, changing 'I've got to get there faster' to 'I'm going fast enough'.), group therapy and psychoanalysis. Research will tell us which if any of these methods is most effective; at present it seems likely that all of them have some favourable effect on Type-A behaviour and on the risk of developing heart disease.[6]

Treatments aimed at changing the over-controlled character of the suppressor-denier have not yet been specifically tested against the outcome most commonly associated with this trait: cancer. Indeed, it is difficult to imagine quite how such a test could be designed so as to be practically and ethically feasible. The antidote to this up-tight way of relating to the world is plain enough: some sort of training or therapy to make the person loosen up, and encouragement, in a social context, of emotional expression and openness. This is very much what many of the traditional psychotherapies are about. Almost all forms of therapy involving groups are founded on the belief that the public expression of feelings and emotions leads to better adjustment and is in itself healthy. In psychoanalysis, a kind of stage is constructed for the playing out of emotional dramas. Old buried fears and needs are dug up and the feelings attached to them are ventilated and worked through.

A recent study by James Pennebaker and his colleagues in Dallas is of particular relevance to the debate about stress and illness.[7] Pennebaker made 50 healthy undergraduate students write at length either about the most upsetting events of their lives or, alternatively, about superficial topics. The writing took place over four consecutive days. Two interesting findings came out of the study. First, compared to the controls, the students who wrote about their life traumas showed improved immune function after the four days of writing and for a subsequent follow-up period of six weeks. Immune competence was measured by the standard method of taking blood samples and assessing the activity of T-cells against a challenge substance simulating an invader, in the laboratory. Students who had written about traumas in their lives also had fewer episodes of sickness, as assessed by visits to the health centre, than did the others. Second, those in the trauma group were asked, 'To what extent did you write about something which you have previously held back telling others?' Those who specifically stated they had written about things they had previously bottled-up showed greater immune improvements than the others. This kind of direct intervention research is very new, but what there is of it looks promising.

Which forms of psychotherapy do better than others?

Of all the different forms of therapy, it is interesting to ask whether there is a clear winner—whether one particular therapy does better than all the others. Broadly speaking, types of therapy can be grouped under two headings: 1) those concerned with a person's emotions, especially the ventilation and understanding of emotions that have become bottled-up; and 2) those that say, forget about emotions and concentrate purely on changing behaviour. The first style of therapy originates from Freud and the psychodynamic school (although there have been many different variations on Freud's original ideas), and the second is a product of the behaviourist school. Behaviourism is a branch of psychology, associated particularly with B. F. Skinner, which ignores emotions and the stream of consciousness and assumes the only profit to be had from therapy is from treating behaviour itself. Its method is modelled on studies with animals which have shown that undesirable forms of behaviour—bad habits—can be changed to good ones by rewarding the good ones and refusing to reward the bad ones. Some modern approaches, such as Attribution Therapies, combine both techniques by encouraging healthier attributions about emotional problems.[8]

About 500 studies have been carried out on the effectiveness of the different forms of psychotherapy. Interestingly, these show that there is very little to choose between them.[9] Behavioural treatments may have the edge over the others in the treatment of phobias and obsessions—which perhaps is not surprising as the problem in both these cases is behaviour that has become stereotyped and out of context—but otherwise treatments seem to be roughly equivalent in their effectiveness. The suggestion has been made that despite their different academic origins and their differences in procedure, these therapies may work through some feature common to all therapeutic encounters. To add to the mystery, treatment with a placebo is almost as effective as treatment using one or other form of accredited therapy! Even more interesting are the 20-odd studies that have been done comparing the effectiveness of trained and untrained therapists: highly trained professionals are no more effective than only briefly trained ones.[9] So if the form of therapy doesn't matter and therapists don't get better with a higher level of training and experience, and yet therapy works, what actually is going on in the therapy session? This question is not answered by any of the traditional theories such as psychoanalysis or behaviourism, because the explanations these offer are opposed.

Holistic treatments

A feeling of dissatisfaction with the way traditional medicine is heading can be sensed in the growing following of what are known as holistic approaches to treatment. The word 'holistic' means 'to take as a whole', and behind the holistic movement is the belief that this is how the body should be conceived and treated in times of mental and physical breakdown. Holistic treatments comprise a mixed bag and include homeopathy, relaxation training, biofeedback, meditation, acupuncture, Tai Chi and faith healing.

Many of these are not particularly new techniques; in fact some of them are very old. But they are only just now beginning to come under the academic spotlight. Now that there is clear evidence of the mutual dependence of the immune system and the brain, and of the effect of stress on immune competence (Chapter 5), the medical and scientific communities are showing an interest. In 1978, the American Holistic Medical Association was founded and in 1983, the British Holistic Medical Association. A new journal, the *British Journal of Holistic Medicine*, started in earnest in 1986.

Favourable outcomes of various kinds have been ascribed to each of these techniques, with varying degrees of scientific justification. Biofeedback involves the measurement of the electrical resistance of the skin using a simple device, known as a galvanic skin response meter (g.s.r.) which attaches to the fingers. Skin resistance varies all the time and is remarkably sensitive to stress and arousal. When a person is stressed or aroused, or even has an emotional thought, skin resistance falls in a characteristic pattern. During biofeedback a person watches the record of his or her own skin resistance level and tries to think relaxing thoughts so that skin resistance stays steady and high. Biofeedback is used as an aid to relaxation training and it has been effective in lowering blood pressure. Moreover, the healthy changes in blood pressure it has caused have been sustained over a period of years and have been associated with a lower rate of heart disease and fewer coronary deaths.[10] In one study, relaxation training was as effective in lowering raised blood pressure as an antihypertensive drug.[11]

Tai Chi is a popular Chinese fitness exercise described as a system of meditation. It involves very gentle movements of the limbs that are repeated over and over again. It is specifically non-energetic and it often takes place in groups. Essentially, it is another version of training a person to relax. Tai Chi has recently been found to cause various chemical changes in the body consistent with improved health—for example, reduced levels of cortisol in the saliva.[12] Cortisol in the bloodstream is a stress hormone known to impair the smooth functioning of the immune system (Chapter 5) and salivary cortisol is generally accepted as an index of cortisol in the blood.

Favourable effects on blood pressure in people with essential hypertension have also been obtained by the laying on of hands, by paranormal healing and by placebos.[13]

Again, what strikes one most about these various treatments is that, like the different forms of psychotherapy, it does not seem to matter very much which one is employed. Exaggerated claims have been made for some treatments, especially by faith healers and the like, which just do not stand up to scientific verification. Nevertheless, evidence is beginning to accumulate that most if not all these procedures can have beneficial effects which are not purely subjective and carry through to chemical and organic changes in the body that affect health. This area of research, understandably, is not very popular within traditional medicine, and traditional medicine controls the funds for doing research. So unfortunately, large-scale prospective and intervention studies of psychological methods of reducing stress and improving health, equivalent to those set up to test drugs and changes in diet, just don't exist.

But why should the various holistic treatments all be roughly the same in their effectiveness, which again seems to be not much of an improvement on the placebo response? The answer, I believe, is the same as the answer to the question, 'Why are all the different forms of psychotherapy roughly equivalent?' All of them are working through the same psychological mechanism: all of them are offering the person social support. The ritual trappings of the treatment may differ, but ritual it is, and being a patient or a client in one of these means becoming caught up in the ritual. Taking a cool look at the assorted happenings that represent these procedures and trying to view them as a man from Mars might, one begins to suspect that the procedure itself—biofeedback, Tai Chi, psychotherapy or whatever—may be no more than an artefact. Just what is involved probably doesn't matter too much. It is not quite right to describe them all as placebos. Something more active is going on than the person passively receiving a treatment: these procedures are effective because they are social repairers. They involve the person and require him or her to participate in a social set-piece, and the act of participation *in itself* is what counts and what is psychologically and physically beneficial.

Participation means *doing* things and it requires a degree of commitment, personal investment and action. The social nature of such commitment is most conspicuous in therapy that takes place in groups. But the same psychological mechanism underpins the efficacy of treatments which it is possible to take home and do by oneself. The essence of the take-home methods is being given something to do by another person—a goal to reach and a set of procedures to go through to reach it that emanate from consensus and hence from some branch of the community. Therein lies the social support and personal challenge and the force drawn as a line in Fig. 18, pushing away from the periphery in towards the centre; towards the sharing of forms.

It must be emphasised that the vital link I am proposing between the individual and the 'social' in no way denies individualism. The individual is not at all the 'product' of the collective. Individuals merely need actively to share structures with others in order for the sense of self, self-esteem and physical health to be sustained. There are millions of original and inspired ways of making yourself look beautiful or smart, and every one of these is unique. But the *idea* of beauty is a cultural idea and one tied to the fashions of time and place. The 1960s emaciated look would not have been understood or appreciated by the Victorians whose ideal was the Rubens woman. Only within a social context does the person have a chance to acquire and exhibit his or her originality and individuality.

THE PUBLIC AND THE POLITICAL

The facts and the analyses presented in the past chapters, as well as bearing on people's everyday lives, also have some important implications for public policy.

Hospitals

At face value hospitals might be thought to offer a secure base and a strong source of social support. The patient is surrounded by other people, the organisation of the ward is bound by a solid routine and the uniforms, the high technology and the extraordinary medical vocabulary are all there to reassure and impress. But what is supported? Certainly not the *person*. The administration supports its own order, it does not support anything else. There is precious little scope for agency, choice and feelings of control over one's destiny from the baleful confinement of one's hospital bed. The whole business could not be designed better to deny the patient these things.

Perhaps this is too harsh a view of the hospital-as-institution. I would not want to be accused of riding rough-shod over the care shown at a personal level by many of the women and men who work at these places. But maybe we have something to learn from the way hospices are consti-tuted and run. Talking to patients is ascribed a central role in the hospice, as is visiting. Pains are taken to see that the patient is kept in touch with the patterns of everyday life rather than cut off from them. There is no subordination of real world personae to the lonely role of the patient as passive recipient of the great technical 'cure'. There is no code of secrecy and medical mystification. Hywel Davies, an American cardiologist, echoes the unease of some of his medical colleagues about the hospital environment, pre-senting the case that in many instances the coronary patient stands a better chance of survival if not moved from his home into the alien surroundings of a hospital.[14]

Whatever the arguments that can be put in favour of the technical care the hospital offers—and it cannot be denied that often these are strong—there can be no justification for the general regard of patients as passive recipients of the administration, as has been handed down through medical tradition. Given the great importance to psychological well-being and physical health of feelings of agency, and the dangers of feeling helpless and alone, one would have thought there are ways of softening the institution a little. Perhaps nothing short of a complete rethink of medical education and the way hospitals are run and organised can change the slot into which patients are automatically put.

However, it is worth bearing in mind the insight of Attribution Theory, that what counts is not so much a person's *actual* choice, but the choice he *feels* he has. There are many ways of structuring situations so that the patient experiences some degree of control over what is happening to him and therefore is permitted to remain like a person.

Retirement

Another important area in which a change in policy could make a critical difference to a person's health is the treatment of the retiring person. In our industrial societies retirement is something of a brutal process. Workers who have devoted the best part of their waking lives to a Company wake up one day suddenly to find they have a new role—the retired person. However blissfully the day of retirement is anticipated, it is an abrupt change and psychologically must be regarded as an acute stress. Professor Leaf, concerned with the process of ageing, expresses these worries about retirement in America:

> The pattern of increasing early retirement in our own society takes a heavy toll of our older citizens. They also find that their offspring generally have neither any room nor any use for them in their urban apartment . . . The devastating effect on the happiness and lifespan of the elderly could be countered at least in part by educational programs to awaken other interests or avocations to which these people could turn in zest when their contribution to the industrial economy is no longer needed. The trend toward shorter worker hours and earlier retirement makes the need for such education urgent.[15]

Professor Leaf wrote this is 1973. Unemployment and early retirement have become much more prominent features of our societies since this time, making the need for the education Leaf wants to see even more urgent.

A more general policy of phased retirement, so that instead of the change from working five days a week to working no days a week, an employee goes from full-time to part-time work, and then on to total retirement, is one step which, if it was adopted as a general policy, would create a breathing space for the necessary coping and adjustment.

Unemployment

There is little that can be added to the findings concerned with the adverse effects on health of unemployment, which were reviewed in Chapter 4. Unemployment causes psychological distress, a deterioration in health and increased mortality. What is more, Professor Iversen's studies of lay-offs from the closure of a large Danish shipbuilder have brought to light a vicious circle. Young people, when they are made redundant, and when this means a drop in standard of living, tend to lose friends and sources of social support.[16] The ideal way to break the circle is, of course, re-employment. The second-best is to reinforce the social support of the unemployed at a personal level and also through community projects. But this is definitely a second-best.

DIET REVISITED: CONCLUSION

This book began with a discussion of diet and the mischievous effects certain dietary substances supposedly have on health. A careful reading of the literature finds hardly any support for the exaggerated claims made and the recommendations given out in so stentorian a fashion by authorities and media alike. For the ordinary person in rough good health, without high blood pressure or raised serum cholesterol, diet is *not* the source of health, any more than are drugs. Smoking and lack of exercise are bad for you. A great excess of anything will poison you. But so long as the diet is adequate and varied, it would seem, barring allergies and food infected with dangerous bugs, you can eat more or less what you want without coming to much harm.

Research on diet and health has reached a kind of stalemate. In contrast, research on stress, coping and illness has come a long way in the last ten to fifteen years, especially with regard to the effects of stress on the immune system. Progress is slow and arduous because it is not possible to draw wide-ranging conclusions from any one study. However, the jig-saw is coming together at last and, taken as a whole, this diverse but now substantial corpus of knowledge leaves no doubt that stress and the psychology of the person hold a crucial key to the understanding of health. This research is given neither the funding nor the publicity that research on diet and drugs gets. Research on diet and drugs is superficially attractive because it is comparatively easy to do, and to interpret and report. But it is based on a naïve optimism: that the key to health is the universally correct diet, and should this perchance fail, the universally correct drug. Medical research claims to be on the threshold of discovering what these are. Not so.

Research on stress, coping and illness is much more difficult, but then human beings are complicated. The signs are getting brighter for a proper place to be given to this corpus of knowledge in medicine. Will it eventually switch the focus of those involved with health away from the traditional version of the organism as a passive collection of organs to that of the person as agent, and a person's health as dependent on a subtle and vital connection with other people?

REFERENCES

INTRODUCTION

1. Lipid Research Clinic Programme. LRC-CPPT results; reduction in incidence of coronary heart disease. *Journal of the American Medical Association*, 1984, 251, 351–364 and 365–74.
2. Consensus Conference. *Journal of the American Medical Association*, 1985, 253, 2080–96.
3. Antoni, M. H. Neuroendocrine influences in psychoimmunology: a review. *Psychology and Health*, 1987, 1, 3–24.

1: BAD THINGS IN THE DIET. SATURATED FATS AND CHOLESTEROL?

1. Ladas, H. S. The war on cancer. I. Victory or deadlock? *Holistic Medicine*, 1988, 3, 91–8.
2. Rosenberg, S. A. Combined modality theory of cancer. *New England Journal of Medicine*, 1985, 312, 1512–4.
3. Walker, C. and Cannon, G. *The Food Scandal*. 1984, London: Arrow Books.
4. Keys, A. Coronary heart disease in seven countries. American Heart Association, Monograph 29. *Circulation*, 1970, 41, Supplement 1.
5. Brisson, G. J. *Lipids in Human Nutrition*. 1982, Lancaster: MTP Press.
6. Cade, J. E., Barker, D.J.P. *et al.* Diet and inequalities in three English towns. *British Medical Journal*, 1988, 296, 1359–62.
7. Gordon, T. Mortality experience among the Japanese in the US, Hawaii and Japan. *Public Health Reports*, 1957, 72, 543–53.
8. Cornfeld, J. and Mitchell, S. Selected risk factors in coronary disease. *Archives of Environmental Health*, 1969, 19, 382–94.

9. Marmot, M. G. and Syme, S. L. Acculturation and coronary heart disease in Japanese-Americans. *American Journal of Epidemiology*, 1976, 104, 225–47.

10. Lyon, J. L. Cardiovascular mortality in Mormons and non-Mormons in Utah 1969–71. *American Journal of Epidemiology*, 1978, 108, 357–65.

11. Cohn, B. A., Kaplan, G. A. and Cohen, R. D. Did early detection and treatment contribute to the decline in ischaemic heart disease mortality? Prospective evidence from the Alameda County Study. *American Journal of Epidemiology*, 1988, 127, 1143–53.

12. Barker, D. J. P. and Osmond, C. Diet and coronary heart disease in England and Wales during and after the second world war. *Journal of Epidemiology and Community Health*, 1986, 40, 37–44.

13. Mann, J. I., Lewis, B. *et al.* Blood lipid concentrations and other cardiovascular risk factors: distribution, prevalence, and detection in Britain. *British Medical Journal*, 1988, 296, 1702–6.

14. Edington, J., Geekie, M. *et al.* Effect of dietary cholesterol on plasma cholesterol in subjects following reduced fat, high fibre diet. *British Medical Journal*, 1987, 294, 333–6.

15. Howard, A. N. and Marks, J. Hypocholesterolaemic effect of milk. *Lancet*, 1977(2), 255–7.

16. Bonanome, A. and Grundy, S. M. Effect of dietary stearic acid on plasma cholesterol and lipoprotein levels. *New England Journal of Medicine*, 1988, 318, 1244–8.

17. MRFIT Research Group. Multiple risk factor intervention trial. *Journal of the American Medical Association*, 1982, 248, 1465–77.

18. World Health Organisation. European collaboration trial of multifactorial prevention of coronary heart disease: final report on the 6-year results. *Lancet*, 1986(1), 869–72.

19. Hjerman, I., Holme, I. *et al.* Effect of diet and smoking intervention on the incidence of coronary heart disease. *Lancet*, 1981(2), 1303–10.

20. Lipid Research Clinical Program. LRC-CPPT results. Reduction in incidence of coronary heart disease. *Journal of the American Medical Association*, 1984, 251, 351–6.

21. Salonen, J. T., Puska, P. *et al.* Decline in mortality from

coronary heart disease in Finland from 1969 to 1979. *British Medical Journal*, 1983, 286, 1857–60.

22. Wilhelmsen, L., Berglund, G. *et al*. The multifactor primary prevention trial in Göteborg, Sweden. *European Heart Journal*, 1986, 7, 279–88.

23. Schatzkin, A., Taylor, P. R. *et al*. Serum cholesterol and cancer in the NHANES I epidemiologic follow-up study. *Lancet*, 1987(2), 298–301. The other two recent large studies are referenced as 24 and 25, this Chapter.

24. See Isles, C. E., Hole, D. J. *et al*. Plasma cholesterol, coronary heart disease, and cancer in the Renfrew and Paisley survey. *British Medical Journal*, 1989, 298, 920–4, for a list of these reports, plus their own report.

25. Knekt, P., Reunanen, A. *et al*. Serum cholesterol and risk of cancer in a cohort of 39,000 men and women. *Journal of Clinical Epidemiology*, 1988, 41, 519–30.

26. Committee of Principal Investigators. A co-operative trial in the primary prevention of ischaemic heart disease using clofibrate. *British Heart Journal*, 1978, 40, 1069–118.

27. Forette, B., Tortrait, D. and Wolmark, Y. Cholesterol as risk factor for mortality in elderly women. *Lancet*, 1989(1), 868–70.

28. A. E. Dugdale. Serum cholesterol and mortality rates. *Lancet*, 1987(1), 155–6.

2: ANOTHER BAD THING IN THE DIET AND SOME GOOD THINGS?

1. UK National Case-control Study Group. Oral contraceptive use and breast cancer risk in young women. *Lancet*, 1989(1), 973–82.

3. Le Fanu, J. *Eat Your Heart Out: The Fallacy of the Healthy Diet*. 1987, London: Macmillan.

3. Kinlen, L. J. Diet and cancer. In R. Cottrell (ed.), *Food and Health*, 1987, Carnforth. Lancs: Parthenon.

4. Enig, M. G., Munn, R. J. and Keeney, M. Dietary fat and cancer trends—a critique. *Federation Proceedings*, 1978, 37, 2215–20.

5. Medical Research Council Working Party. MRC trial of

treatment of mild hypertension: principal results. *British Medical Journal*, 1985, 291, 97–104.

6. Henry, J. P. and Cassel, J. C. Psychosocial factors in essential hypertension. Recent epidemiologic and animal experimental evidence. *American Journal of Epidemiology*, 1969, 90, 171–200.

7. Timio, M., Verdecchia, P. *et al*. Blood pressure changes over 20 years in nuns in a secluded order. *Journal of Hypertension*, 1985, Supplement 3, S387–S388.

8. Henry, J. P. Stress, salt and hypertension. *Social Science and Medicine*, 1988, 26, 293–302.

9. Heagerty, A. M. Salt and blood pressure—a review. In R. Cottrell (ed.) *Food and Health*, 1987. Carnforth, Lancs: Parthenon.

10. Miller, J. Z., Weinberger, M. H. *et al*. Heterogeneity of blood pressure response to sodium restriction in normatensive adults. *Journal of Chronic Diseases*, 1987, 40, 245–50.

11. Murray, R. H., Luft, F. C. *et al*. Blood pressure responses to extremes of sodium intake in normal man. *Proceedings of the Society of Experimental Biology and Medicine*. 1978, 159, 432–6.

12. Intersalt Co-operative Research Group. Intersalt: an international study of electrolyte excretion and blood pressure. Results for 24 hour urinary sodium and potassium excretion. *British Medical Journal*, 1988, 297, 319–28.

13. Australian National Health and Medical Research Council Dietary Salt Study Management Committee. Fall in blood pressure with moderate reduction in salt intake in mild hypertension. *Lancet*, 1989(1) 399–402.

14. Taken from Macdonald, I. Fibre: too much speculation, not enough facts. In D. Anderson (ed.). *A Diet of Reason: Sense and Nonsense in the Healthy Eating Debate*. 1986, London: Social Affairs Unit.

15. For a good and understandable explanation of the different types of fats; also of the nature of transunsaturated fats, and details of the Secondary Prevention Studies, see Brisson, G. J. *Lipids in Human Nutrition: an Appraisal of Dietary Concepts*. 1981, Lancaster: MTP Press.

16. Thomas, L. H. and Winter, J. A. Ischaemic heart disease and consumption of hydrogenated marine oils. *Human Nutrition: Food Sciences and Nutrition*, 1987, 41F, 153–65.

17. Thomas, L. H., Winter, J. A. and Scott, R. G. Concentration of transunsaturated fatty acids in the adipose body tissue of decedents dying of ischaemic heart disease compared with controls. *Journal of Epidemiology and Community health*, 1983, 37, 22–4.

18. Wood, D. A., Butler, S. *et al*. Linoleic and eicosapentaenoic acids in adipose tissue and platelets and risk of coronary heart disease. *Lancet*, 1987(1), 177–82.

19. Schacky, C. von. Porphylaxis of atherosclerosis with marine omega-3 fatty acids. *Annals of Internal Medicine*, 1987, 107, 890–9.

20. Brisson, G. J., 1981, *op. cit.* ref. 15 above.

21. Endres, S., Ghorbani, R. *et al*. The effects of dietary supplementation with n-3 polyunsaturated fatty acids on the synthesis of interleukin-1 and Tumour Necrosis Factor by mononuclear cells. *New England Journal of Medicine*, 1989, 320, 265–71.

22. See Anderson, D. (ed.) *A Diet of Reason: Sense and Nonsense in the Healthy Eating Debate*. 1986, London: Social Affairs Unit.

3: PERSONALITY AND ILLNESS

1. Burch, P. R. J. Ischaemic heart disease: epidemiology, risk factors and cause. *Cardiovascular Research*, 1980, 14, 307–38.

2. Munzarova, M. and Kovarik, J. Is cancer a macrophage-mediated autoaggressive disease? *Lancet*, 1987(1), 952–4.

3. Luborsky, L., Docherty, J. P. and Penick, S. Onset conditions for psychosomatic symptoms. *Psychosomatic Medicine*, 1973, 35, 187–204.

4. Irwin, M. Depression and immune function. *Stress Medicine*. 1988, 4, 95–103.

5. Persky, V. W., Kempthorne-Rawson, J. *et al*. Personality and risk of cancer: 20 year follow-up of the Western Electric Study. *Psychosomatic Medicine*, 1987, 49, 435–49.

6. Kissen, D. M. The significance of personality in lung cancer in men. *Annals of the New York Academy of Sciences*, 1966, 125, 820–6.

7. Bahnson, M. S. and Bahnson, C. B. Ego defenses in cancer patients. *Annals of the New York Academy of Sciences*, 1969, 164, 319–34.

8. See Dixon, N. F. *Preconscious Processing*, 1981, Chichester: Wiley.

9. Greer, S. and Morris, T. Psychological attributes of women who develop breast cancer. *Journal of Psychosomatic Research*, 1975, 19, 147–53.

10. Wirsching, M., Stierlin, H. *et al*. Psychological identification of breast cancer patients before biopsy. *Journal of Psychosomatic Research*, 1982, 26, 1–10.

11. Derogatis, L., Abeloff, M. and Melisaratos, N. Psychological coping mechanisms and survival time in metastatic breast cancer. *Journal of the American Medical Association*, 1979, 242. 1504–8.

12. Jensen, M. R. Psychobiological factors predicting the course of breast cancer. *Journal of Personality*, 1987, 55, 317–42.

13. Antoni, M. H. and Gookin, K. Host moderator variables in the promotion of cervical neoplasia—I personality facets. *Journal of Psychosomatic Research*, 1988, 32, 327–38.

14. Thomas, C., Turner, P. and Madden, F. Coping and the outcome of stoma surgery. *Journal of Psychosomatic Research*, 1988, 32, 457–67.

15. See Borysenko, J. Z. Healing motives: an interview with David McClelland. *Advances*, 1985, 2, 29–41.

16. Antoni, M. H. Neuroendocrine influences in psychoimmunology and neoplasia: a review. *Psychology and Health*, 1987, 1, 3–24.

17. Jamner, L. D., Schwartz, G. E. and Hoyle, L. The relationship between repressive and defensive coping styles and monocyte, eosinophile, and serum glucose levels: support for the opioid peptide hypothesis of repression. *Psychosomatic Medicine*, 1988, 50, 567–75.

18. Gross, J. Emotional expression in cancer onset and progression. *Social Science and Medicine*, 1989, 28, 1239–48.

19. Frey, W. H., DeSota-Johnson, D. *et al*. Effects of stimulus on the chemical composition of human tears. *American Journal of Opthalmology*, 1981, 92, 559–67.

20. Grossarth-Maticek, R. Siegrist, J. and Vetter, H. Interpersonal repression as a predictor of cancer. *Social Science and Medicine*, 1982, 16, 493–8.

21. Goldstein, H. S., Edelberg, R. *et al*. Relationship of resting

blood pressure and heart rate to experienced and expressed anger. *Psychosomatic Medicine*, 1989, 50, 321–9.

22. Morris, J. N., Heady, J. A. *et al.* Coronary heart disease and the physical activity of work. *Lancet*, 1953(2), 1903–7, 1111 –20.

23. Friedman, M. and Rosenman, R. H. *Type-A Behavior and Your Heart*. 1974, New York: Alfred Knopf.

24. Jenkins, C. D., Zyzanski, S. J. and Rosenman, R. H. Progress toward validation of a computer scored test for the Type-A coronary prone behavior pattern. *Psychosomatic Medicine*, 1971, 33, 193–202.

25. Matthews, K. A. and Haynes, S. G. Type-A behavior pattern and coronary disease risk. *American Journal of Epidemiology*, 1986, 123, 923–61.

26. Rosenman, R. H., Brand, R. J. and Jenkins, C. D. Coronary heart disease in the Western Collaborative Group Study. Final follow-up experience of eight and a half years. *Journal of the American Medical Association*, 1975, 233, 872–7.

27. Hecker, M. H. L., Chesney, M. A. *et al.* Coronary-prone behaviors in the Western Collaborative Study. *Psychosomatic Medicine*, 1988, 50, 153–64.

28. Ragland, D. R. and Brand, R. J. Coronary heart disease mortality in the Western Collaborative Group Study. Follow-up experience of 22 years. *American Journal of Epidemiology*, 1988, 127, 462–75.

29. Shoham-Yakuborich, I., Ragland, D. R. *et al.* Type-A behavior pattern and health status after 22 years of follow-up in the Western Collaborative Group Study. *American Journal of Epidemiology*, 1988, 128, 579–88.

30. Haynes, S. G. and Feinleib, M. Type-A behavior and the incidence of coronary heart disease in the Framingham Heart Study. *Advances in Cardiology*, 1982, 29, 85–95.

31. Matthews, K. A. Psychological perspectives on the Type-A behavior pattern. *Psychological Bulletin*, 1982, 91, 293–323.

32. French-Belgium Collaborative Group. Ischaemic heart disease and psychological patterns. Prevalence and incidence studies in Belgium and France. *Advances in Cardiology*, 1982, 29, 25–31.

33. Barefoot, J. C., Dahlstrom, W. G. and Williams, R. B.

Hostility, coronary heart disease incidence and total mortality: a 25 year follow-up study of 255 physicians. *Psychosomatic Medicine*, 1983, 45, 59–63.

34. Shekelle, R., Gale, M. and Ostfeld, A. Hostility, risk of coronary heart disease and mortality. *Psychosomatic Medicine*, 1983, 45, 59–63. See also Koskenvuo, M., Kaprio, J. *et al.* Hostility as a risk factor for mortality and ischaemic heart disease in men. *Psychosomatic Medicine*, 1988, 50, 330–40.

35. Langeluddecke, P., Fulcher, G. *et al.* Type-A behaviour and coronary atherosclerosis. *Journal of Psychosomatic Research*, 1988, 32, 77–84.

36. Williams, R. B., Barefoot, J. C. *et al.* Type-A behavior and angiographically documented coronary atherosclerosis in a sample of 2,289 patients. *Psychosomatic Medicine*, 1988, 50, 139–52.

37. Patel, C., Marmot, M. G. *et al.* Trial of relaxation in reducing coronary risk: four years follow-up. *British Medical Journal*, 1985, 290, 1103–6.

38. Patel, C. and Marmot, M. G. Can general practitioners use training in relaxation and management of stress to reduce mild hypertension? *British Medical Journal*, 1988, 296, 21–4.

39. Nunes, E. V., Frank, K. A. and Kornfeld, D. S. Psychologic treatment for the Type-A behavior pattern and for coronary heart disease: a meta-analysis of the literature. *Psychosomatic Medicine*, 1987, 48, 159–73.

40. Lehnert, H., Kaluza, K. *et al.* Long-term effects of a complex behavioral treatment of essential hypertension. *Psychosomatic Medicine*, 1987, 49, 422–30.

41. Wrześniewski, K., Wonicki, J. and Turlejski, J. Type-A behavior pattern and illness other than coronary heart disease. *Social Science and Medicine*, 1988, 27, 623–6. Also, Valdes, M. and de Flores, T. Type-A behavior and vulnerability to diseases: a Spanish retrospective study. *Stress Medicine*, 1987, 3, 135–40.

42. The Review Panel on coronary-prone behavior and coronary heart disease. *Circulation*, 1981, 63, 1199–215.

43. See also Boman, B. Stress and heart disease. In S. Fisher and J. Reason (eds) *Handbook of Life Stress, Cognition and Health*, 1988, Chichester: Wiley.

44. See Ornstein, R. and Sobel, D. *The Healing Brain*, 1988,

London: Macmillan. Also Totman, R. G. *Social Causes of Illness*, 1987, London: Souvenir Press.

45. See Totman, R. G. *op. cit.* ref. 44 above. Also Keltikangas-Jarvinen, L. and Jokinen, J. Type-A behavior, coping mechanisms and emotions related to somatic risk factors of coronary heart disease in adolescents. *Journal of Psychosomatic Research*, 1989, 33, 17–29.

46. Bruhn, J. G., Paredes, A. *et al.* Psychological predictors of sudden death in myocardial infarction. *Journal of Psychosomatic Research*, 1974, 18, 187–91.

47. A philosophical perspective shared by the American philosopher, C. Whitbeck and the Finnish philosopher, I. Pron. See Nordenfelt, L. Health and disease: two philosophical perspectives. *Journal of Epidemiology and Community Health*, 1986, 41, 281–4.

4: Stressful situations and illness

1. Bourne, P. G. *Men, Stress and Vietnam*. 1970, Boston Mass.: Little Brown.

2. See Sereny, G. *Into That Darkness* (trans. R. Seaver). 1974, London: Weidenfeld and Nicolson.

3. Antonovsky, A. *Health, Stress and Coping*. 1979, London: Josey-Bass.

4. A collation and analysis of survivors' accounts is to be found in Des Pres, T. *The Survivors, an Anatomy of Life in the Death Camps*. 1976, New York: Oxford University Press.

5. Hart, K. *I am Alive*. 1962, London: Abelard Schuman.

6. Bettelheim, B. *The Informed Heart*. 1961, London: Thames and Hudson.

7. Frankl, V. E. *From Death Camp to Existentialism* (trans. Ilse Lasch). 1959, Boston: Beacon.

8. Zywulska, K. *I Came Back* (trans. K. Cenkalska). 1951, London: Dennis Dobson.

9. Levi, P. *If This is a Man. The Truce*. 1979, London: Penguin. Note—one of the key texts about life in the camps.

10. Fisher, S. Leaving home. In S. Fisher and J. Reason (eds) *Handbook of Life Stress, Cognition and Health*. 1988, Chichester: Wiley.

11. Galvão-Teles, A. and Sampaio, D. Psychologically determined death in anorexia nervosa. *Lancet*, 1987(1), 1097.

12. Phillips, D. P. and King, E. W. Death takes a holiday: mortality surrounding major social occasions. *Lancet*, 1988(2), 728–32.

13. Stroebe, W., Stroebe, M. S. *et al*. The effects of bereavement on mortality: a social psychological analysis. In J. R. Eiser (ed.) *Social Psychology and Behavioral Medicine*. 1982, London: Wiley.

14. Cochrane, R. Marriage, separation and divorce. In S. Fisher and J. Reason (eds), *Handbook of Life Stress, Cognition and Health*. 1988, Chichester: Wiley.

15. Brown, G. W. and Harris, T. *Social Origins of Depression*. 1978, London: Tavistock.

16. Rowland, K. F. Environmental events predicting death for the elderly. *Psychological Bulletin*, 1977, 349–72.

17. Clegg, F. Bereavement. In S. Fisher and J. Reason (eds) *Handbook of Life Stress, Cognition and Health*. 1988, Chichester: Wiley.

18. Parkes, C. M. Bereavement: studies of grief in adult life. 1972, London: Tavistock.

19. Rahe, R. H. and Lind, E. Psychosocial factors and sudden cardiac death. *Journal of Psychosomatic Research*, 1971, 15, 19–24.

20. Freud, S. *The Psychopathology of Everyday Life*. 1960, London: Hogarth Press.

21. Tabachnick, N. *Accident or Suicide? Destruction by Automobile*. 1973, Springfield, Ill.: Charles C. Thomas.

22. Holinger, P. C. and Klemen, E. H. Violent deaths in the United States 1900–1975. *Social Science and Medicine*, 1982, 16, 1929–38.

23. Schmale, A. H. and Iker, H. P. The psychological setting of uterine cervical cancer. *Annals of the New York Academy of Sciences*, 1966, 125, 807–13. Engel, G. L. Psychological stress, vasodepressor (vasovagal) syncope, and sudden death. *Annals of Internal Medicine*, 1978, 89, 403–13. Also, Mandler, G. *Mind and Emotion*. 1975, New York: Wiley.

24. Chambers, W. N. and Reiser, H. F. Congestive heart failure. *Psychosomatic Medicine*, 1953, 39–60.

25. Mei-Tal, V., Meyerowitz, S. and Engel, G. L. The role of

psychological process in a somatic disorder: multiple sclerosis. *Psychosomatic Medicine*, 1970, 32, 67–86.

26. Seligman, M. E. P. *Helplessness: on Depression, Development and Death*. 1975, San Francisco: Freeman.

27. Jacobs, M. A., Silken, A. Z. *et al*. Life stress and respiratory illness. *Psychosomatic Medicine*, 1970, 32, 233–43.

28. Moss, S. *Illness, Immunity and Social Interaction*. 1973, New York: Wiley.

29. Stroebe, W. and Stroebe, M. S. 1982, *op. cit.* ref. 13 above.

30. Iversen, L., Andersen, O. *et al*. Unemployment and mortality in Denmark. *British Medical Journal*, 1987, 295, 879–84.

31. Jackson, P. R. and Warr, P. Mental health of unemployed men in different parts of England and Wales. *British Medical Journal*, 1987, 295, 525.

32. Kessler, R. C., House, J. S. and Turner, J. B. Unemployment and health in a community sample. *Journal of Health and Social Behavior*, 1987, 28, 51–9.

33. Fryer, D. The experience of unemployment in social context. In S. Fisher and J. Reason (eds). *Handbook of Life Stress, Cognition and Health*. 1988, Chichester: Wiley.

34. Westin, S., Norum, D. and Schlesselman, J. J. Medical consequences of a factory closure: illness and disability in a four-year follow-up study. *International Journal of Epidemiology*, 1988, 17, 153–61.

35. Moser, K. A., Goldblatt, P. O. *et al*. Unemployment and mortality: Comparison of the 1971 and 1981 longitudinal study census samples. *British Medical Journal*, 1987, 294, 86–90.

36. Jahoda, M. *Employment and Unemployment*. 1982, Cambridge: Cambridge University Press.

5: STRESS, THE BODY AND THE IMMUNE SYSTEM

1. Old, L. J. Tumor necrosis factor. *Scientific American*, 1988, 258, 41–9.

2. Balkwill, F. The body's protein weapons. *New Scientist*, 1988, 16th June (Inside Science no. 12), 1–4.

3. Dinarello, C. A. and Meir, J. W. Interleukins. *American Review of Medicine*, 1986, 37, 173–8.

4. Greer, S. and Brady, M. Natural killer cells: one possible link

between cancer and the mind. *Stress and Illness*, 1988, 4, 105–11.

5. Munzarová, M. and Kovarík, J. Is cancer a macrophage-mediated autoaggressive disease? *Lancet*, 1987(1), 952–4.

6. Camara, E. G. and Danao, T. C. The brain and the immune system: a psychosomatic network. *Psychosomatics*, 1989, 30, 140–5.

7. Irwin, M. Depression and immune function. *Stress Medicine*, 1988, 4, 95–103.

8. *Lancet* (editorial). Depression, stress and immunity. 1987(1), 1467–8.

9. Baker, G. H. B. Psychological factors and immunity. *Journal of Psychosomatic Research*, 1987, 31, 1–10.

10. Bartrop, R. W., Luckhurst, E. *et al.* Depressed lymphocyte function after bereavement. *Lancet*, 1977(1), 834–6.

11. Annotation: Stress, the immune system and mental illness. *Stress Medicine*, 1987, 3, 257–8.

12. Locke, S. E., Kraus, L. *et al.* Life change, stress, psychiatric symptoms and natural killer cell activity. *Psychosomatic Medicine*, 1984, 46, 441–53.

13. Kiecolt-Glaser, J. K., Ricker, D. *et al.* Urinary cortisol levels, cellular immunocompetency, and loneliness in psychiatric inpatients. *Psychosomatic Medicine*, 1984, 46, 15–23.

14. Kiecolt-Glaser, J. K., Garner, W. *et al.* Psychosocial modifiers of immunocompetence in medical students. *Psychosomatic Medicine*, 1984, 46, 7–14.

15. Jamner, L. D. Schwartz, G. E. and Leigh, H. The relationship between repressive and defensive coping styles and monocyte, eosinophile, and serum glucose levels: support for the opioid peptide hypothesis of repression. *Psychosomatic Medicine*, 1988, 50, 567–75.

16. Kiecolt-Glaser, J. K., Glaser, R. *et al.* Psychosocial enhancement of immunocompetence in a geriatric population. *Health Psychology*, 1985, 4, 25–41.

17. Arnetz, B. B., Wasserman, J. *et al.* Immune function in unemployed women. *Psychosomatic Medicine*, 1987, 49, 3–11.

18. Kiecolt-Glaser, J. K., Fisher, L. *et al.* Marital quality, marital disruption and immune function. *Psychosomatic Medicine*, 1987, 49, 13–33.

19. Kiecolt-Glaser, J. K., Kennedy, S. *et al.* Martial discord,

and immunity in males. *Psychosomatic Medicine* 1988, 50, 213–29.

20. Totman, R. G., Kiff, J. *et al.* Predicting experimental colds in volunteers from different measures of recent life stress. *Journal of Psychosomatic Research*, 1980, 24, 155–63.

21. See also Cox, T. Psychobiological factors in stress and health. In S. Fisher and J. Reason (eds) *Handbook of Life Stress, Cognition and Health*, 1988, Chichester: Wiley.

22. Antoni, M. H. Neuroendocrine influences in psychoimmunology and neoplasia: a review. *Psychology and Health*, 1987, 1, 3–24.

23. Schlesser, M. A., Winokur, G. and Sherman, B. Hypothalamic-pituitary-adrenal axis activity in depressive illness. *Archives of General Psychiatry*, 1980, 35, 737–43.

24. Zis, A. P. Opioidergic regulation of hypothalamo-pituitary-adrenal function in depression and Cushing's disease: an interim report. *Psychoneuroendocrinology*, 1988, 13, 419–30.

25. Besedeovsky, H. O., Sorkin, E. *et al.* Hypothalamic changes during the immune response. *European Journal of Epidemiology*, 1977, 7, 325–8. Besedeovsky, H. O., del Ray, A. and Sorkin, E. What do the brain and the immune system know about each other? *Immunology Today*, 1983, 4, 342–6.

26. See Ornstein, R. and Sobel, D. *op. cit.* Chapter 3, ref. 44.

27. See Solomon, G. F. The emerging field of psychoneuroimmunology. *Advances*, 1985(2) 6–19. Also Ader, R. (ed.) *Psychoneuroimmunology*, 1981, New York: Academic Press.

28. Duesberg, P. Retroviruses as carcinogens and pathogens: expectations and reality. *Cancer Research*, 1987, 47, 1199–2200. See also Adams, J. *AIDS: The HIV Myth*. 1989, London: Macmillan.

29. Farzadegan, H., Polis, M. A. *et al.* Loss of immunodeficiency virus type I (HIVI) antibodies with evidence of viral infection in asymptomatic homosexual men. *Annals of Internal Medicine*, 1988, 108, 785–90.

30. Patel, C. *Fighting Heart Disease*. 1987, London: Dorling Kindersley.

31. See Monagan, D. Sudden death. *Discover*, 1986, 7, 64–71. Also Ornstein, R. and Sobel, D. 1988, *op. cit.* Chapter 3, ref. 44.

32. Lane, R. D. and Schwartz, G. E. Induction of lateralized

sympathetic input to the heart by the CNS during emotional arousal: a possible neurophysiologic trigger of sudden cardiac death. *Psychosomatic Medicine*, 1987, 49, 274–83.

33. See, for example, Burch, P. R. J. Ischaemic heart disease: epidemiology, risk factors and cause. *Cardiovascular Research*, 1980, 14, 307–38.

34. See for example, Gleick, J. *Chaos: Making a New Science*. 1988, London: Heinemann.

6: THE HEALTH-GIVING NATURE OF SOCIAL SUPPORT

1. Cobb, S. Social support as a moderator of life stress. *Psychosomatic Medicine*, 1976, 38, 300–14.

2. Caplan, G. Mastery of stress: psychological aspects. *American Journal of Psychiatry*, 1981, 138, 413–20.

3. Hammer, M. 'Core' and 'extended' social networks in relation to health and illness. *Social Science and Medicine*, 1983, 17, 405–11.

4. Leavy, R. Social support and psychological disorder: a review. *Journal of Community Psychology*, 1983, 11, 3–21.

5. Schwarzer, R. and Leppin, A. Social support and health: a meta-analysis. *Psychology and Health*, 1989, 3, 1–15.

6. Berkman, L. F. and Syme, S. L. Social networks, host resistance, and mortality: a nine-year follow-up study of Alameda County residents. *American Journal of Epidemiology*, 1979, 109, 186–204.

7. Orth-Gomér, K. and Johnson, J. V. Social network interaction and mortality: a six-year follow-up study of a random sample of the Swedish population. *Journal of Chronic Diseases*, 1987, 40, 949–57.

8. Jylhä, M. and Aro, S. Social ties and survival among the elderly in Tampere, Finland. *International Journal of Epidemiology*, 1989, 18, 158–64.

9. Reed, D., McGee, D. *et al*. Social networks and coronary heart disease among Japanese men in Hawaii. *American Journal of Epidemiology*, 1983, 117, 384–96.

10. Kaplan, G. A., Salonen, J. T. *et al*. Social connections and mortality from all causes and from cardiovascular disease: prospective evidence from Eastern Finland. *American Journal of Epidemiology*, 1988, 128, 370–80.

11. See, for example, Seeman, T. E. and Syme, S. L. Social networks and coronary artery disease: a comparison of the structure and function of social relations as predictors of disease. *Psychosomatic Medicine*, 1987, 49, 341–54.

12. Funch, D. P. and Marshall, J. The role of stress, social support and age in survival from breast cancer. *Journal of Psychosomatic Research*, 1983, 27, 77–83.

13. Hagburg, B. and Malmquist, A. A prospective study of patients in chronic hemiodialysis—IV. Pre-treatment psychiatric and psychological variables predicting outcome. *Journal of Psychosomatic Research*, 1974, 18, 315–19.

14. Brown, G. W. and Harris, T. *Social Origins of Depression*, 1978, London: Tavistock.

15. Raphael, B. Preventive intervention with the newly bereaved. *Archives of General Psychiatry*, 1977, 34, 1450–4.

16. Sosa, R., Kennell, J. *et al*. The effect of a supportive companion on perinatal problems, length of labor, and mother-infant interaction. *New England Journal of Medicine*, 1980, 303, 597–600.

17. Arnetz, B. B., Theorell, T. *et al*. An experimental study of social isolation in elderly people: psychoendocrine and metabolic effects. *Psychosomatic Medicine*, 1983, 45, 395–406.

18. Spiegel, D., Kraemer, H. C. *et al*. Effect of psychosocial treatment on survival of patients with metastatic breast cancer. *Lancet*, 1989 (2), 888–91.

19. See House, J. S. *Work, Stress and Social Support*, 1981, Reading MA: Addison-Wesley.

20. Blumenthal, J., Burg, M. M. *et al*. Social support, Type-A behavior, and coronary artery disease. *Psychosomatic Medicine*, 1987, 49, 331–40.

21. Tousignant, M. and Maldonado, M. Sadness, depression and social reciprocity in highland Ecuador. *Social Science and Medicine*, 1989, 28, 899–904.

22. Sterling, P. and Eyer, I. Biological basis of stress-related mortality. *Social Science and Medicine*, 1981, 15E, 3–42.

23. Antonovsky, A. *Health, Stress and Coping*. 1979, San Francisco: Josey-Bass.

24. Wolcott, D. L., Wellisch, D. K. *et al*. serum gastrin and the family environment in duodenal ulcer. *Psychosomatic Medicine*, 1981, 43, 501–6.

25. Grossarth-Maticek, R., Siegrist, J. and Vetter, H. Interpersonal repression as a predictor of cancer. *Social Science and Medicine*, 1982, 16, 493–8.

26. O'Reilly, P. and Thomas, H. E. Role of support networks in maintenance of improved cardiovascular health status. *Social Science and Medicine*, 1989, 28, 249–60.

27. Schwenck, T. L. and Hughes, C. C. The family as patient in family medicine: rhetoric or reality? *Social Science and Medicine*, 1983, 17, 1–6.

28. Cassel, J. C. Social science theory as a source of hypotheses in epidemiological research. *American Journal of Public Health*, 1964, 54, 1482–8.

29. Comstock, G. W. and Partridge, K. B. Church attendance and health. *Journal of Chronic Diseases*, 1972, 25, 665–72.

30. Caplan, G. 1981, *op. cit.* ref. 2 above.

31. Troyer, H. Review of cancer among 4 religious sects: evidence that life-styles are distinctive sets of risk factors. *Social Science and Medicine*, 1988, 26, 1007–17.

32. Timio, M., Verdecchia, P. *et al.* 1985, *op. cit.* Chapter 2, ref. 7.

33. Henry, J. P. and Cassel, J. C. Psychosocial factors in essential hypertension. Recent epidemiologic and animal experimental evidence. *American Journal of Epidemiology*, 1969, 90, 171–200.

34. Leaf, A. Getting Old. *Scientific American*, 1973, 229, 44–52.

35. Gallagher, B. J. *The Source of Mental Illness*. 1980, Englewood Cliffs: Prentice-Hall. See also Kuo, W. Theories of migration and mental health: an empirical testing on Chinese Americans. *Social Science and Medicine*, 1976, 10, 297–306.

36. Marks, R. A review of empirical findings. In S. L. Syme and L. G. Reeder (eds) *Social Stress and Cardiovascular Disease: Milbank Memorial Fund Quarterly*, 1967, 45.

37. Durkheim, E. *Suicide*. 1952, London: Routledge and Kegan Paul.

38. Marmot, M. G. and Syme, S. L., 1976, *op. cit.* Chapter 1, ref. 9.

39. Ornstein, R. and Sobel, D. *The Healing Brain*, 1988, London: Macmillan.

40. Schulz, R. *The Psychology of Death, Dying and Bereavement*, 1978, Reading MA: Addison-Wesley.

41. Schulz, R. and Brenner, G. Relocation of the aged: a review

and theoretical analysis. *Journal of Gerontology*, 1977, 32, 323–33.

42. Gore, S. The effect of social support in moderating the health consequences of unemployment. *Journal of Health and Social Behavior*, 1978, 19, 157–65.
43. Nuckolls, K. B., Cassel, J. C. and Kaplan, B. H. Psychological assets, life crises and the prognosis of pregnancy. *American Journal of Epidemiology*, 1972, 95, 431–41.
44. *Lancet* (editorial). People need people. 1988(2), 886.
45. Friedman, E., Katcher, A. *et al*. Animal companions and one-year survival of patients after discharge from a coronary care unit. *Public Health Reports*, 1980, 95, 307–12.

7: STRESS AND DISCONNECTEDNESS

1. Seeman, T. E. and Syme, S. L., 1987, *op. cit.* Chapter 6, ref. 11.
2. Jylhä, M. and Aro, S., 1989, *op. cit.* Chapter 6, ref. 8.
3. Harré, R. *Social Being*. 1979, Oxford: Blackwell.
4. Also Levi, P., 1979, *op. cit.* Chapter 4, ref. 9.
5. Totman, R. G. Cognitive dissonance in the placebo response—a pilot experiment. *British Journal of Medical Psychology*, 1976, 49, 393–400.
6. Benson, H. and McCallie, D. P. Angina pectoris and the placebo effect. *New England Journal of Medicine*, 1979, 300, 1424–9. See also Beecher, H. K. Surgery as placebo: a quantitative study of bias. *Journal of the American Medical Association*, 1961, 176, 1102–7.
7. For example, Findlay, T. The placebo and the physician. *Medical Clinics of North America*, 1953, 1821–6. Also Totman, R. G. *Social Causes of Illness*, 1987, London: Souvenir Press.
8. Frank, J. The faith that heals. *Johns Hopkins Medical Journal*, 1975, 137, 127–31.
9. Shapiro, A. K. The placebo effect in the history of medical treatment: implications for psychiatry. *American Journal of Psychiatry*, 1959, 116, 298–304.
10. Janet, P. M. Psychological healing. A historical and clinical study (trans. E. and C. Paul). 1925, London: Macmillan.
11. Rotter, J. B. Generalized expectancies for internal vs.

external control of reinforcement. *Psychological Monographs*, 1966, 80 (1, Whole no. 609).

12. Garber, J. and Seligman, M. E. P. (eds) *Human Helplessness: Theory and Applications*, 1980, London: Academic Press.

13. Hewstone, M. (ed.) *Attribution Theory*. 1983, Oxford: Blackwell.

14. Antaki, C. and Brewin, C. (eds) *Attributions and Psychological Change*. 1982, London: Academic Press.

15. Peterson, C. In C. Antaki and C. Brewin, 1982, *op. cit.* ref. 14 above.

16. Searle, J. R. *Speech Acts*. 1969. Westford MA: Murray.

17. See Sturrock, J. (ed.) *Structuralism and Since*. 1979, Oxford: Oxford University Press.

18. Jupp, T. C., Roberts, C., and Cook-Gumperz, J. J. Language and disadvantage: the hidden process. In J. J. Gumperz (ed.) Language and Social Identity, 1982, Cambridge: Cambridge University Press.

19. Wittgenstein, L. *Philosophical Investigations*, 1953, Oxford: Blackwell.

20. Wittgenstein, L. *The Blue and Brown Books*. 1958, Oxford, Blackwell.

21. Maddi, S. R. and Kobasa, S. C. *The Hardy Executive: Health Under Stress*, 1984, Homewood, Ill.: Dow Jones-Irwin.

22. See Breuer, G. *Sociobiology and the Human Dimension*. 1982, Cambridge: Cambridge University Press.

23. For an elaboration of these arguments and their implications see Totman, R. G. *Social and Biological Roles of Language*, 1985, London: Academic Press.

8: COPING AND STAYING HEALTHY

1. Butler, R. N. The life review: an interpretation of reminiscence in the aged. In R. Kastenbaum (ed.). *New Thoughts on Old Age*. 1964, New York: Springer.

2. Kovel, J. *A Complete Guide to Therapy*. 1981, New York: Pantheon.

3. Kohn, M. L. Occupational structure and alienation. *American Journal of Sociology*, 1976, 82, 111–30.

4. Alfredsson, L., Karasek, R. and Theorell, T. Myocardial infarction risk and psycho-social work environment: an

analysis of the male Swedish working force. *Social Science and Medicine*, 1982, 16, 463–7.

5. For an explanation of this point, see Totman, R. G. The philosophical foundations of attribution therapies. In C. Antaki and C. Brewin (eds), *Attributions and Psychological Change*, 1982, London: Academic Press.

6. Nunes, E. V. *et al.* 1987, *op. cit.* Chapter 3, ref. 39.

7. See Pennebaker, J. W. Confiding traumatic experiences and health. In S. Fisher and J. Reason (eds), *Handbook of Life Stress, Cognition and Health*. 1988, Chichester: Wiley.

8. See Antaki, C. and Brewin, 1982, *op. cit.* Chapter 7, ref. 14. Also Garber, J. and Seligman, M. E. P. 1980, *op. cit.* Chapter 7, ref. 12.

9. Howarth, I. and Dussuyer, I. D. Helping people cope with the long-term effects of stress. In S. Fisher and J. Reason (eds) *Handbook of Life Stress, Cognition and Health*, 1988, Chichester: Wiley.

10. Patel, C. and Marmot, M. G. 1988, *op. cit.* Chapter 3, ref. 38.

11. MRC Working Party, 1985, *op. cit.* Chapter 2, ref. 5.

12. Jin, P. Changes in heart rate, noradrenaline, cortisol and mood during Tai Chi. *Journal of Psychosomatic Research*, 1989, 33, 197–206.

13. Buetler, J. J., Attevelt, J. T. M. *et al.* Paranormal healing and hypertension. *British Medical Journal*, 1988, 296, 1491–4.

14. Davies, H. *Modern Medicine. A Doctor's Dissent.* 1977, London: Abelard Schuman.

15. Leaf, A. 1973, *op. cit.* Chapter 6, ref. 34.

16. Sabroe, S. and Iversen, I. Unemployment, social support, psychological well-being, and psychosomatic symptoms. In B. Starrin, P-G. Svensson and H. Wintersberger (eds.) *Unemployment, Poverty and Quality of Working Life.* 1988: published by the World Health Organisation. See also, Iversen, I. Unemployment and mortality. *Stress Medicine*, 1989, 5, 85–92.

INDEX